Cambridge
BEC Preliminary
3

WITH ANSWERS

*Examination papers from
University of Cambridge
ESOL Examinations:
English for Speakers of
Other Languages*

CAMBRIDGE UNIVERSITY PRESS
Cambridge, New York, Melbourne, Madrid, Cape Town, Singapore, São Paulo

Cambridge University Press
The Edinburgh Building, Cambridge CB2 2RU, UK

www.cambridge.org
Information on this title: www.cambridge.org/9780521671958

© Cambridge University Press 2006

It is normally necessary for written permission for copying to be obtained in advance from a publisher. The candidate answer sheets at the back of this book are designed to be copied and distributed in class. The normal requirements are waived here and it is not necessary to write to Cambridge University Press for permission for an individual teacher to make copies for use within his or her own classroom. Only those pages which carry the wording '© UCLES 2006 Photocopiable' may be copied.

First published 2006

Printed in the United Kingdom at the University Press, Cambridge

ISBN-13 978-0521-671958 Student's Book with answers
ISBN-10 0-521-671957 Student's Book with answers

ISBN-13 978-0521-671989 Audio Cassette
ISBN-10 0-521-671981 Audio Cassette

ISBN-13 978-0521-671972 Audio CD
ISBN-10 0-521-671973 Audio CD

ISBN-13 978-0521-671965 Self-study Pack
ISBN-10 0-521-671965 Self-study Pack

Contents

Thanks and acknowledgements iv

Introduction 1

Test 1 Reading and Writing 16
Listening 32
Speaking 39

Test 2 Reading and Writing 42
Listening 58
Speaking 65

Test 3 Reading and Writing 68
Listening 84
Speaking 91

Test 4 Reading and Writing 94
Listening 110
Speaking 117

Key (including tapescripts and sample answers)
Test 1 120
Test 2 125
Test 3 130
Test 4 135

Speaking test interlocutor frames 141

Sample Answer Sheets 142

Thanks and acknowledgements

The authors and publishers are grateful to the following for permission to use copyright material in *BEC Preliminary 3*. While every effort has been made, it has not been possible to identify the sources of all the material used and in such cases the publishers would welcome information from the copyright owners.

p. 24: For the adapted extract 'Should you let your pastime go full-time?' by Alexander Garrett, *Management Today Magazine*, March 2002; p. 48: Adapted extract 'Why seeing is succeeding' by Professor W Chan Kim and Renée Mauborgne, the authors of an International Bestseller book Blue Ocean Strategy (HBSP 2005). Adapted from a *Financial Times* article; p. 50: Adapted extract 'Giving up the day job' by Wendy Ledger, *Evening Standard*, July 2001; p. 74: Adapted extract 'Massive Attack' by Kate Hilpern. Used by kind permission of the author; p. 76: Adapted extract 'Insurer targeted fast set' by Mark Stretton, *The Sunday Times*, © Mark Stretton/News International Syndication, London, 4 March 2001; p. 102: Adapted extract 'DFS feels benefit of rates and strong pound' by Sally Patten, *The Times*, © Sally Patten/News International Syndication, London, 15 October 1999.

Introduction

TO THE STUDENT

This book is for candidates preparing for the Cambridge Business English Certificate Preliminary examination. It contains four complete tests based on past papers.

The BEC Suite

The Business English Certificates (BEC) are certificated examinations which can be taken on various dates throughout the year at approved Cambridge BEC centres. They are aimed primarily at individual learners who wish to obtain a business-related English language qualification, and provide an ideal focus for courses in Business English. Set in a business context, BEC tests English language, not business knowledge. BEC is available at three levels – Preliminary, Vantage and Higher.

The BEC Suite is linked to the five ALTE/Cambridge levels for language assessment, and to the Council of Europe's Framework for Modern Languages. It is also aligned with the UK Qualifications and Curriculum Authority's National Standards for Literacy, within the National Qualifications Framework (NQF).

BEC	Equivalent Main Suite Exam	Council of Europe Framework Level	UK NQF Level
	Certificate of Proficiency in English (CPE)	C2 (ALTE Level 5)	
BEC Higher	Certificate in Advanced English (CAE)	C1 (ALTE Level 4)	Level 2*
BEC Vantage	First Certificate in English (FCE)	B2 (ALTE Level 3)	Level 1
BEC Preliminary	Preliminary English Test (PET)	B1 (ALTE Level 2)	Entry 3
	Key English Test (KET)	A2 (ALTE Level 1)	

* This represents the level typically required for employment purposes to signify the successful completion of compulsory secondary education in the UK.

BEC Preliminary

The BEC Preliminary examination consists of three papers:

Reading and Writing	1 hour 30 minutes
Listening	40 minutes (approximately)
Speaking	12 minutes

Introduction

Test of Reading and Writing (1 hour 30 minutes)

The **Reading** section of the Reading and Writing paper consists of seven parts with 45 questions, which take the form of two multiple matching tasks, four multiple choice tasks, and a form-filling or note completion task. Part 1 contains five very short texts, Part 2 contains one short text, and Part 3 contains graphs, charts or tables. Parts 4, 5 and 6 each contain one longer text. Part 7 contains two short texts. The texts are mainly taken from newspapers, business magazines, business correspondence, books, leaflets, brochures, etc. They are all business-related, and are selected to test a wide range of reading skills and strategies.

For the **Writing** section of the Reading and Writing paper, candidates are required to produce two pieces of writing. For Part 1, they write a note, message, memo or email to a colleague or colleagues within the company. For Part 2, they write a piece of business correspondence to somebody outside the company.

Candidates are asked to write 30 to 40 words for Part 1 and 60 to 80 words for Part 2. For Part 1, assessment is based on achievement of task. For Part 2, assessment is based on achievement of task, range and accuracy of vocabulary and grammatical structures, organisation, content, and appropriacy of register and format.

Test of Listening (approximately 40 minutes)

This paper consists of four parts with 30 questions, which take the form of two multiple choice tasks and two note completion tasks. Part 1 contains eight very short conversations or monologues, Part 2 contains a short conversation or monologue, Part 3 contains a monologue, and Part 4 contains one longer text. The texts are audio-recordings based on a variety of sources including interviews, telephone calls, face-to-face conversations and documentary features. They are all business-related, and are selected to test a wide range of listening skills and strategies.

Test of Speaking (12 minutes)

The Speaking test consists of three parts, which take the form of an interview section, a short presentation on a business topic, and a discussion. In the standard test format, candidates are examined in pairs by two examiners: an interlocutor and an assessor. The assessor awards a mark based on the following four criteria: Grammar and Vocabulary, Discourse Management, Pronunciation and Interactive Communication. The interlocutor provides a global mark for the whole test.

Marks and results

The three BEC Preliminary papers total 120 marks, after weighting. Each skill (Reading, Writing, Listening and Speaking) is weighted to 30 marks. A candidate's overall grade is based on the total score gained in all three papers. It is not necessary to achieve a satisfactory level in all three papers in order to pass the examination. Pass grades are Pass with Merit and Pass. The minimum successful performance in order to achieve a Pass corresponds to about 65% of the total marks. Narrow Fail and Fail are failing grades. Every candidate is provided with a Statement of Results, which includes a graphical display of their performance in each skill. These are shown against the scale Exceptional – Good – Borderline – Weak and indicate the candidate's relative performance in each paper.

TO THE TEACHER

Candidature

Each year BEC is taken by over 70,000 candidates throughout the world. Most candidates are either already in work or studying in preparation for the world of work.

Content, preparation and assessment

Material used throughout BEC is as far as possible authentic and free of bias, and reflects the international flavour of the examination. The subject matter should not advantage or disadvantage certain groups of candidates, nor should it offend in areas such as religion, politics or sex.

TEST OF READING

Part	Main Skill Focus	Input	Response	No. of questions
1	Reading – understanding short, real-world notices, messages, etc.	Notices, messages, timetables, adverts, leaflets, etc.	Multiple choice	5
2	Reading – detailed comprehension of factual material; skimming and scanning skills	Notice, list, plan, contents page, etc.	Matching	5
3	Reading – interpreting visual information	Graphs, charts, tables, etc. (The information may be presented in eight separate graphics or combined into a composite graphic.)	Matching	5
4	Reading for detailed factual information	Longer text (approx. 150–200 words): article, business letter, product description, report, minutes, etc.	Right/Wrong/ Doesn't say	7
5	Reading for gist and specific information	Longer text (approx. 300–400 words): newspaper or magazine article, advert, report, leaflet, etc.	Multiple choice	6
6	Reading – grammatical accuracy and understanding of text structure	Longer text (approx. 125–150 words): newspaper or magazine article, advert, leaflet, etc.	Multiple choice cloze	12
7	Reading and information transfer	Short memos, letters, notices, adverts, etc.	Form-filling, note completion	5

Introduction

Reading Part One

In this part there are five short texts, each of which is accompanied by a multiple choice question containing three options. In all cases the information will be brief and clear and the difficulty of the task will lie not in understanding context but in identifying or interpreting meaning.

A wide variety of text types, representative of the world of international business, can appear in this part. Each text will be complete and have a recognisable context.

Preparation
In order to prepare for this part it would be useful to expose students to a wide range of notices and short texts taken from business settings. It is also useful to practise answering sample questions, asking students to explain why the answer is correct (and why the two incorrect options do not apply).

Reading Part Two

This is a matching task comprising one text and five questions, which are often descriptions of people's requirements. Candidates are required to match each question to an appropriate part of the text labelled A–H. (As there are only five questions, some of the labels are redundant.) The testing focus of this part is vocabulary and meaning.

Preparation
For preparation purposes, students need to be familiar with text types that are divided into lists, headings or categories; for example, the contents page of a directory or book, the plan of an office, the departments in a business or shop, or the items in a catalogue. Many of the questions in this part require a simple interpretation of what the parts of the text mean and preparation for this could involve setting students real-world tasks of this kind using authentic (but simple) sources.

Reading Part Three

This task consists of eight graphs or charts (or one or more charts or graphs with eight distinct elements) and five questions. Each question is a description of a particular visual and candidates are expected to match the questions to their corresponding graphs, which are labelled A–H.

Preparation
This part focuses on understanding trends and changes. Candidates need to be able to interpret graphic data and understand the language used to describe it. Expressions such as 'rose steadily', 'remained stable', 'decreased slowly' and 'reached a peak' should be introduced to students, along with relevant topics, such as sales of goods, share price movement and monthly costs.

Reading Part Four

This task is a text accompanied by seven, three-option multiple choice items. Each question presents a statement and candidates are expected to indicate whether the statement is A 'Right' or B 'Wrong' according to the text, or whether the information is not given in the text (C 'Doesn't say'). Candidates will not be expected to understand every word in the text but they should be able to pick out salient points and infer meaning where words in the text are unfamiliar. The questions will refer to factual information in the text but candidates will be required to do some processing in order to answer the questions correctly.

Preparation
This can be a difficult task for candidates who are not familiar with the three choices represented by A, B and C, and who might not understand the difference between a statement that is incorrect and one that depends on information that is not provided in the text. Students need to be trained to identify a false statement, which means that the opposite or a contradictory statement is made in the text, and to recognise that this is not the same as a statement that is not covered in the text (for which an alternative answer might be 'Don't know').

Reading Part Five

This part presents a single text accompanied by six multiple choice comprehension items. The text is informative and is often taken from a leaflet, or from a newspaper or magazine article.

Candidates are expected to employ more complex reading strategies in this task, in that they should demonstrate their ability to extract relevant information, to read for gist and detail, to scan the text for specific information, and to understand the purpose of the writer and the audience for which the text is intended.

Preparation
In preparing candidates for this part, it would be a good idea to expose them to a variety of texts of a similar length. As texts become longer, slow readers are at a disadvantage and some practice in improving reading speed would be beneficial for this part. It would also be useful to discuss the following areas:
- the title
- the topic
- the writer's purpose
- the theme or main idea of each paragraph
- factual details that can be found in the text
- the writer's opinions (if they are evident).

Reading Part Six

This is a multiple choice cloze test. Candidates have to select the correct word from three options to complete twelve gaps. This part has a predominantly grammatical focus and tests candidates' understanding of the general and detailed meaning of a text and in particular their ability to analyse structural patterns.

Introduction

Preparation
Any practice in the grammatical and structural aspects of the language is useful in preparing students for this part. However, it is equally important for students to analyse the structure and coherence of language within longer discourse so that they are encouraged to read for meaning beyond the sentence level. As tasks such as this typically focus on common grammatical difficulties, it it also useful to ask students to analyse the errors in their own work. Pairwork activities might be productive as students can often help each other in the areas of error identification and analysis.

Reading Part Seven

Candidates are given two short texts, for example a memo and an advertisement, and are asked to complete a form based on this material. There are five gaps, which should be completed with a word, a number or a short phrase. In this part, candidates are tested on their ability to extract relevant information and complete a form accurately.

For this part, candidates need to transfer their answers in capital letters to an Answer Sheet.

Marks

One mark is given for each correct answer. The total score for Reading is then weighted to 30 marks.

TEST OF WRITING

Part	Functions/Communicative Task	Input	Response	Register
1	e.g. (re-)arranging appointments, asking for permission, giving instructions	Rubric only (plus layout of output text type)	Internal communication (medium may be note, message, memo or email) (30–40 words)	Neutral/ formal/ informal
2	e.g. apologising and offering compensation, making or altering reservations, dealing with requests, giving information about a product	One piece of input, which may be business correspondence (medium may be letter, fax or email), internal communication (medium may be note, memo or email), notice, advert, etc. (plus layout of output text type)	Business correspondence (medium may be letter, fax or email) (60–80 words)	Neutral/ formal

For BEC Preliminary, candidates are required to produce two pieces of writing:
- an internal company communication; this means a piece of communication with a colleague or colleagues within the company on a business-related matter, and the delivery medium may be a note, message, memo or email;

- a piece of business correspondence; this means correspondence with somebody outside the company (e.g. a customer or supplier) on a business-related matter, and the delivery medium may be a letter, fax or email.

Writing Part One

Candidates are asked to produce a concise piece of internal company communication of between 30 and 40 words, using a written prompt. The text will need to be produced in the form of a note, message, memo or email, and candidates are given guidance on the layout of memos and emails. The reason for writing and target reader are specified in the rubric, and bullet points explain what content points have to be included. Relevant ideas for one or more of these points will have to be 'invented' by the candidate.

Writing Part Two

Candidates are asked to produce an extended piece of business correspondence of between 60 and 80 words. This task involves the processing of a short text, such as a letter or advertisement, in order to respond to it. A number of bulleted content points below the text clearly indicate what should be included in the answer. Some of this information will need to be 'invented' by the candidate.

Although the use of some key words is inevitable, candidates should not 'lift' phrases from the question paper to use in their answers. This may be penalised.

Preparing for the Writing questions

In preparing students for the Writing tasks it would be beneficial to familiarise them with a variety of business correspondence. Analysing authentic correspondence would help students understand better how to structure their answer and the type of language to use. When doing this, it would be useful to focus on the following areas:
- the purpose of the correspondence
- references to previous communication
- factual details
- the feelings and attitude of the writer
- the level of formality
- the opening sentence
- the closing sentence
- paragraphing
- the desired outcome.

If students are in a class, it might be possible to ask them to write and reply to each other's correspondence so that they can appreciate the importance of accurate content.

In a similar fashion, internal company memos and messages might also be written and analysed in terms of the above so that students can recognise the different levels of formality involved. It is a necessary part of preparing for the test that students understand the uses of, and styles inherent in, different types of business communication so that they are aware of how and why different types of correspondence are used.

Introduction

Assessment

An impression mark is awarded to each piece of writing. The general impression mark scheme is used in conjunction with a task-specific mark scheme, which focuses on criteria specific to each particular task. This summarises the content, organisation, register, format and target reader indicated in the task.

For Part 1, examiners use the mark schemes primarily to assess task achievement. For Part 2, examiners use the mark schemes to assess both task achievement **and** language.

The band scores awarded are translated to a mark out of 5 for Part 1 and a mark out of 10 for Part 2. The total score for Writing is then weighted to 30 marks.

Both general impression mark schemes are interpreted at Council of Europe Level B1.

Summaries of the general impression mark schemes are reproduced below. Examiners work with a more detailed version, which is subject to regular updating.

General mark scheme for Writing Part One

Band	
5	**Very good attempt** at task, achieving all content points.
4	**Good attempt** at task, achieving all content points.
3	**Satisfactory attempt** at task, achieving all content points with some effort by the reader, or achieving two content points.
2	**Inadequate attempt** at task, achieving one content point, possibly with noticeable irrelevance.
1	**Poor attempt** at task; no content points achieved, has little relevance.
0	No relevant response or too little language to assess.

General mark scheme for Writing Part Two

Band	
5	Full realisation of the task set. • All four content points achieved. • Confident and ambitious use of language; errors are minor, due to ambition, and non-impeding. • Good range of structure and vocabulary. • Effectively organised, with appropriate use of simple linking devices. • Register and format consistently appropriate. Very positive effect on the reader.
4	Good realisation of the task set. • Three or four content points achieved. • Ambitious use of language; some non-impeding errors. • More than adequate range of structure and vocabulary. • Generally well organised, with attention paid to cohesion. • Register and format on the whole appropriate. Positive effect on the reader.
3	Reasonable achievement of the task set. • Three content points achieved. • A number of errors may be present, but are mostly non-impeding. • Adequate range of structure and vocabulary. • Organisation and cohesion are satisfactory, on the whole. • Register and format reasonable, although not entirely successful. Satisfactory effect on the reader.
2	Inadequate attempt at the task set. • Two or three content points achieved. • Numerous errors, which sometimes impede communication. • Limited range of structure and vocabulary. • Content is not clearly organised or linked, causing some confusion. • Inappropriate register and format. Negative effect on the reader.
1	Poor attempt at the task set. • One or two content points achieved. • Serious lack of control; frequent basic errors. • Little evidence of structure and vocabulary required by task. • Lack of organisation, causing a breakdown in communication. • Little attempt at appropriate register and format. Very negative effect on the reader.
0	Achieves nothing. Either fewer than 25% of the required number of words or totally illegible or totally irrelevant.

Introduction

TEST OF LISTENING

Part	Main Skill Focus	Input	Response	No. of questions
1	Listening for specific information	Short conversations/ monologues	3-option multiple choice	8
2	Listening for specific information	Short telephone conversation/ prompted monologue	Gap-filling (numbers and spellings)	7
3	Listening for specific information	Monologue	Note-taking (content words)	7
4	Listening for gist/specific information	Conversation/interview/ discussion between two or more people	3-option multiple choice	8

Listening Part One

The eight questions in this part of the paper are three-option multiple choice questions. For each question, candidates hear a short conversation or monologue, typically lasting around 15 to 30 seconds. Each monologue or dialogue is repeated on the recording in order to give candidates a chance to check their answer. The multiple choice options may be textual or they may be in the form of pictures, graphs or diagrams.

In the extracts in Part 1, candidates are being tested on their understanding of spoken English used in a range of situations and on their ability to extract factual information. They may need to pick out a name or time or place. Alternatively, they may have to identify a trend in a graph or a place on a map or the location of an object in a room. In every case, it will be necessary for candidates to follow the conversation closely.

Listening Part Two

This part consists of a short conversation or monologue, typically lasting around a minute and a half, which contains factual information. On the question paper there is a form, table, chart or set of notes with seven gaps where information is missing. Candidates have to complete each of the gaps. This part has a numerical focus and the answers may include dates, prices, percentages or figures.

Listening Part Three

Candidates hear a monologue. On the question paper there is a set of notes or a form with gaps. There are seven gaps to complete and the answers may be one or two words. On occasion, the key to one of the gaps may be a date.

Listening Part Four

This part, which lasts about three minutes, contains a longer listening text which generally takes the form of an interview, or a discussion between two or possibly more speakers. There are eight, three-option multiple choice questions on the question paper and these are always in a written format. In this part of the Listening component, candidates are being tested on their ability to understand the gist of a longer text and extract detailed and specific information as required by the questions. They may also be tested on the speakers' opinions.

At the end of the Listening test, candidates have ten minutes to transfer their answers to their Answer Sheet.

Preparing for the Listening paper

The Listening component is carefully paced and candidates are tested on short extracts in Part 1, so that they can gradually 'tune in' to the spoken language and improve their listening skills without losing their place in the test.

Listening can be a very demanding activity and candidates should practise their listening skills regularly using a wide variety of listening sources. Candidates who enter the Listening test having done this will be at an advantage.

At BEC Preliminary level, it is advisable to collect as much listening material as possible that is suitably paced and of an appropriate length. Native speakers speak at many different speeds and some speak much more clearly than others. If it is possible to collect a bank of authentic material that is carefully chosen, this would prove useful practice for students. Otherwise, it might be better to make use of specially designed materials for this level.

For Part 1, candidates should try to listen to short extracts of speech concentrating on understanding the general idea or main points of what is said. For Parts 2 and 3, practice should be given in note-taking. Prior to hearing tapes or audio materials, students should be given details of the information they need to listen for. Teachers should discuss the task with the students beforehand and encourage them to listen for cues and prompts that will help them identify the points they need to find. When listening to longer texts, it would also be useful to discuss areas such as:
- the purpose of the speech or conversation
- the speakers' roles
- the speakers' opinions
- the language functions being used
- factual details
- conclusions.

Marks

One mark is given for each correct answer, giving a total score of 30 marks for the whole Listening paper.

TEST OF SPEAKING

Part	Format/Content	Time	Interaction Focus
1	Conversation between the interlocutor and each candidate General interaction and social language	About 2 minutes	The interlocutor encourages the candidates to give information about themselves and to express personal opinions.
2	A 'mini presentation' by each candidate on a business theme Organising a larger unit of discourse Giving information and expressing opinions	About 5 minutes	Each candidate is given prompts which they use to prepare and give a short talk on a business-related topic.
3	Two-way conversation between candidates followed by further prompting from the interlocutor Expressing opinions, agreeing and disagreeing	About 5 minutes	The candidates are presented with a scenario supported by visual or written prompts which generates a discussion. The interlocutor extends the discussion with further spoken prompts.

The Speaking test is conducted by two oral examiners (an interlocutor and an assessor), with pairs of candidates. The interlocutor is responsible for conducting the Speaking test and is also required to give a mark for each candidate's performance during the whole test. The assessor is reponsible for providing an analytical assessment of each candidate's performance and, after being introduced by the interlocutor, takes no further part in the interaction.

The Speaking test is designed for pairs of candidates. However, where a centre has an uneven number of candidates, the last three candidates will be examined together.

Speaking Part One

In the first part of the test, the interlocutor addresses each candidate in turn and asks questions about where they work or study, where they live or what they do in their free time. The questions will be slightly different for each candidate and candidates will not be addressed in strict sequence. This part of the test takes about two minutes and during this time candidates are tested on their ability to talk briefly about themselves, to provide information on subjects such as their home, hobbies and jobs, and to perform simple functions such as agreeing and disagreeing, and expressing preferences.

Speaking Part Two

The second part of the test is a 'mini presentation'. Candidates are asked to speak for about one minute on a business-related topic. At Preliminary level candidates are given two topics from which they should choose one. Each topic is presented as a main focus with three bullet points. Candidates are given one minute to prepare the talk (both candidates or group of three prepare at the same time). After each candidate finishes speaking the next candidate is asked which of the bullet points they think is the most important. This part of the test focuses on the candidate's ability to present basic ideas and organise a longer piece of discourse.

Speaking Part Three

The third part of the test is a discussion between candidates. The interlocutor outlines a scenario and provides prompts by way of black and white pictures or written prompts to help the candidates. The candidates are asked to speak for about two minutes. The interlocutor will support the conversation as appropriate and then ask further questions related to the main theme. This part of the test focuses on the candidate's ability to interact appropriately using a range of linguistic skills.

Preparing for the Speaking test

It is important to familiarise candidates with the format of the test before it takes place, by the use of paired activities in class. Teachers may need to explain the benefits of this type of assessment to candidates. The primary purpose of paired assessment is to sample a wider range of discourse than can be elicited from an individual interview.

In the first part of the test, candidates mainly respond to questions or comments from the interlocutor. In the second part, candidates are given the opportunity to produce an extended piece of discourse and to demonstrate an ability to maintain a longer speech turn. In the third part, they are required to interact more actively, taking turns appropriately, asking and answering questions and negotiating meaning. To prepare for this part, it is a good idea to encourage students to change partners in class so that they grow accustomed to interacting with a variety of people, some of whom they do not know so well.

For all parts of the test, students need to practise the exchange of personal and non-personal information, and prompt materials will be needed to help them do this. Teachers could prepare a selection of these for each part of the test. Students could discuss the materials as a class group prior to engaging in pairwork activities. Such activities would familiarise students with the types of interactive skills involved in asking and providing factual information, such as: speaking clearly, formulating questions, listening carefully and giving precise answers.

Assessment

Candidates are assessed on their own performance and not in relation to each other according to the following analytical criteria: Grammar and Vocabulary, Discourse Management, Pronunciation and Interactive Communication. These criteria are interpreted at Preliminary level. Assessment is based on performance in the whole test and is not related to particular parts of the test.

Introduction

Both examiners assess the candidates. The assessor applies detailed, analytical scales, and the interlocutor applies a Global Achievement Scale, which is based on the analytical scales. The analytical criteria are further described below.

Grammar and Vocabulary

This refers to range and accuracy as well as the appropriate use of grammatical and lexical forms. At BEC Preliminary level, a range of grammar and vocabulary is needed to deal with the tasks. At this level, candidates may make frequent minor errors and use some inappropriate vocabulary, but this should not obscure intended meanings.

Discourse Management

This refers to the coherence, extent and relevance of each candidate's individual performance. Contributions should be adequate to deal with the BEC Preliminary level tasks.

Pronunciation

This refers to the candidate's ability to produce comprehensible utterances. At BEC Preliminary level, most meanings are conveyed through the appropriate use of stress, rhythm, intonation and clear individual sounds.

Interactive Communication

This refers to the candidate's ability to take an active part in the development of the discourse. At BEC Preliminary level, candidates are able to take turns and sustain the interaction by initiating and responding appropriately.

Global Achievement Scale

This refers to the candidate's overall performance throughout the test. Throughout the Speaking test, candidates are assessed on their language skills and, in order to be able to make a fair and accurate assessment of each candidate's performance, the examiners must be given an adequate sample of language to assess. Candidates must, therefore, be prepared to provide full answers to the questions asked by either the interlocutor or the other candidate, and to speak clearly and audibly. While it is the responsibility of the interlocutor, where necessary, to manage or direct the interaction, thus ensuring that both candidates are given an equal opportunity to speak, it is the responsibility of the candidates to maintain the interaction as much as possible.

Grading and results

Grading takes place once all scripts have been returned to Cambridge ESOL and marking is complete. This is approximately five weeks after the examination. There are two main stages: grading and awards.

Grading

The three papers total 120 marks, after weighting. Each skill represents 25% of the total marks available. The grade boundaries (Pass with Merit, Pass, Narrow Fail and Fail) are set using the following information:
- statistics on the candidature
- statistics on the overall candidate performance
- statistics on individual items, for those parts of the examination for which this is appropriate (Reading and Listening)
- the advice of the Principal Examiners, based on the performance of candidates, and on the recommendation of examiners where this is relevant (Writing)
- comparison with statistics from previous years' examination performance and candidature.

A candidate's overall grade is based on the total score gained in all three papers. It is not necessary to achieve a satisfactory level in all three papers in order to pass the examination.

Awards

The Awarding Committee deals with all cases presented for special consideration, e.g. temporary disability, unsatisfactory examination conditions, suspected collusion, etc. The Committee can decide to ask for scripts to be re-marked, to check results, to change grades, to withhold results, etc. Results may be withheld because of infringement of regulations or because further investigation is needed. Centres are notified if a candidate's results have been scrutinised by the Awarding Committee.

Results

Results are reported as two passing grades (Pass with Merit and Pass) and two failing grades (Narrow Fail and Fail). The minimum successful performance which a candidate typically requires in order to achieve a Pass corresponds to about 65% of the total marks. Candidates are given Statements of Results which, in addition to their grades, show a graphical profile of their performance on each paper. These are shown against the scale Exceptional – Good – Borderline – Weak and indicate the candidate's relative performance in each paper. Certificates are issued to passing candidates after the issue of Statements of Results and there is no limit on the validity of the certificate.

Further information

For more information about BEC or any other Cambridge ESOL examination write to:

Cambridge ESOL Information
1 Hills Road
Cambridge CB1 2EU
United Kingdom

Tel: +44 1223 553355
Fax: +44 1223 460278
email: ESOL@ucles.org.uk
website: www.CambridgeESOL.org

In some areas, this information can also be obtained from the British Council.

Test 1

READING AND WRITING   1 hour 30 minutes

READING

PART ONE

Questions 1–5

- Look at questions **1–5**.
- In each question, which sentence is correct?
- For each question, mark one letter (**A**, **B** or **C**) on your Answer Sheet.

Example: 0

Telephone message

Bill Ryan caught 9.30 flight – due here 11.30 now, not 12.30.

When does Bill Ryan expect to arrive?

A   9.30
B   11.30
C   12.30

The correct answer is **B**, so mark your Answer Sheet like this:

| 0 | A | B | C |

1

> Add any comments to our proposal in pencil – these will then be discussed at the next committee meeting.

The meeting will consider

A   the company's plans for the future.
B   the performance of the committee.
C   suggested changes to a document.

2

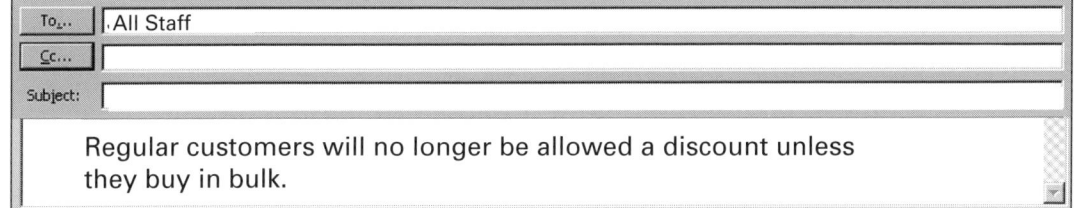

To...: All Staff
Cc...:
Subject:

Regular customers will no longer be allowed a discount unless they buy in bulk.

- **A** Discounts will be offered to regular customers on orders of any size.
- **B** Established customers will only qualify for price reductions on large orders.
- **C** Customers can continue to get a discount if they place orders frequently.

3

> Tom,
> Arrange with printers for 3 cm logos to be increased in size by 10% on next brochure order.

Tom must contact the printers to

- **A** change a design detail.
- **B** make arrangements for collection.
- **C** request a greater quantity.

4

BOOKSTORE

To: Office Staff/Customer Orders Department
From: Ted Smith/Warehouse Manager

Due to stock relocation, orders already placed will not be despatched between June 3 and June 10.

- **A** Office staff will transfer to a new location on June 10.
- **B** Warehouse workers should remove out-of-date stock by June 10.
- **C** Customers have to wait until after June 10 for recent orders.

5

 TRAINING COURSE

Questionnaires available from Information Desk. Please complete and hand in at Reception.

R. Hughes
Training Manager

Trainees are asked to leave completed forms

- **A** at the Information Desk.
- **B** with the Training Manager.
- **C** with the Reception staff.

Test 1

PART TWO

Questions 6–10

- Look at the notice below. It shows a list of stands at a trade fair.
- For questions **6–10**, decide which stand (**A–H**) each person on the opposite page needs to visit.
- For each question, mark one letter (**A–H**) on your Answer Sheet.
- Do not use any letter more than once.

TRADE FAIR STANDS

A *CIP System*: Internal Telephone Systems

B *Bertix plc*: Top-of-the-Range Portable Computers

C *Aurora Ltd*: Hands-Free Mobile Phones for Vehicles

D *FastCo Ltd*: Distribution Services

E *Tops Recruitment Agency*: Specialists in Management

F *HTML Ltd*: Website Marketing and Internet Advertising

G *Journey.com*: Travel Agency for the Business Executive

H *FTA*: Finance for Training

6 Sally Green imports computer hardware and needs a company to transport it from the port to her chain of stores.

7 In order to obtain an advanced business qualification, Paul White has to take a year off work without pay, and is looking for funding.

8 John Brown is buying new vans for his service engineers and wants to be able to contact them at any time.

9 When travelling on business, Ben Smith needs to be able to write letters, send emails and analyse data.

10 Sophie Jones wants professional help in finding good candidates for senior posts in her computer software company.

Test 1

PART THREE

Questions 11–15

- Look at the chart below. It shows how a company has recruited new staff over a ten-year period.
- Which year does each sentence (**11–15**) on the opposite page describe?
- For each sentence, mark one letter (**A–H**) on your Answer Sheet.
- Do not use any letter more than once.

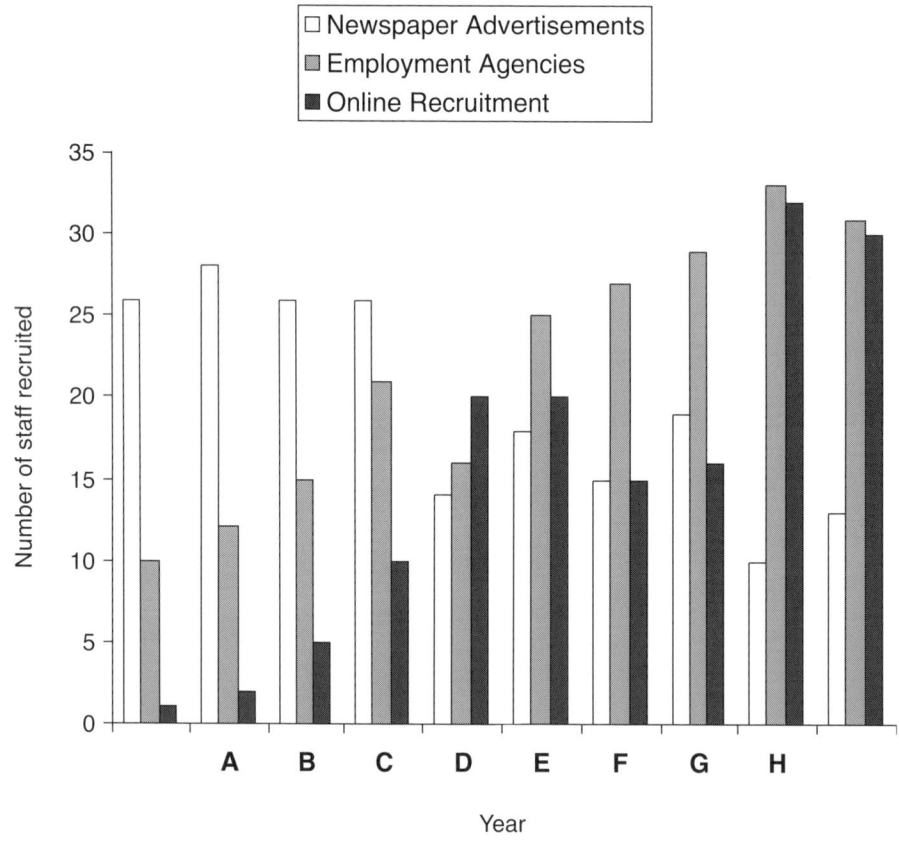

11 There was a slight drop in the use of newspaper adverts on the previous year, while both agency and online recruitment continued to rise.

12 This year more staff were recruited through agencies than either newspaper or online adverts but both these methods experienced an increase on the previous year.

13 There was an increase in both employment agency and online recruitment on the previous year although recruitment through newspaper adverts fell sharply.

14 Fewer employees were recruited through newspaper adverts this year than the previous year and online recruitment also declined.

15 This year the number of candidates recruited online was double the figure for the previous year, while the numbers recruited through employment agencies fell slightly.

PART FOUR

Questions 16–22

- Read the article below about the UK cycle industry.
- Are sentences **16–22** on the opposite page 'Right' or 'Wrong'? If there is not enough information to answer 'Right' or 'Wrong', choose 'Doesn't say'.
- For each sentence (**16–22**), mark one letter (**A, B** or **C**) on your Answer Sheet.

CYCLES MOVE WITH THE TIMES

Times have been hard for the UK cycle industry. Poor weather and competition from abroad have had a serious effect on sales. Manufacturers have had to cut back and last month more than 40 job losses were announced at Cycle World, one of the country's main bicycle factories in Leicester. But the company says it is fighting to win back customers, using such strategies as improved after-sales and bikes built to specific customer requirements.

Two years ago, Cycle World sold off its bike-making machinery in an effort to cut costs and save money. The company's Leicester factory is now only an assembly plant as most of the parts are imported.

The company produces half a million bikes a year across the full Cycle World range, with nearly all of these being sold in the UK. Production is largely done by hand. Workers use the batch production method – everyone making up to 600 bikes of a particular model at any one time.

At the height of its success, Cycle World employed 7,000 people but, like many areas of manufacturing, it has since shrunk. Its 1950s purpose-built factory now employs just 470 permanent workers, with numbers rising to 700 as temporary staff are taken on to meet seasonal demands in sales.

16 The weather has encouraged more people to buy bikes.

    A Right   **B** Wrong   **C** Doesn't say

17 Management have recently had to make people redundant at Cycle World.

    A Right   **B** Wrong   **C** Doesn't say

18 Cycle World is providing a more personal service to regain market share.

    A Right   **B** Wrong   **C** Doesn't say

19 Cycle World imported some bike-making machinery as part of a cost-cutting exercise.

    A Right   **B** Wrong   **C** Doesn't say

20 The majority of Cycle World bicycles are sold to the domestic market.

    A Right   **B** Wrong   **C** Doesn't say

21 Only a small number of different bike models are produced each month.

    A Right   **B** Wrong   **C** Doesn't say

22 700 extra staff are taken on at the busiest time of year.

    A Right   **B** Wrong   **C** Doesn't say

PART FIVE

Questions 23–28

- Read the article below about starting a business.
- For each question (**23–28**) on the opposite page, choose the correct answer.
- Mark one letter (**A, B** or **C**) on your Answer Sheet.

Enjoying your career

'My business is my hobby,' someone tells you. 'I wish I could make a living from my hobby,' you may think. 'It sounds ideal.'

Yet according to Sue Cole, a management expert, there can be both advantages and disadvantages for those who combine their hobby with their career. 'There's a real possibility that your hobby becomes less attractive when it's your job. But also quite a few people who make their hobby their career become too enthusiastic and forget about the basic principles of business,' she says. 'For example, someone may think: "I love cooking. There aren't enough restaurants in this area. I'll start one up." And they go ahead without establishing how many customers they'll need each day or what income they'll require to cover costs. That can be a recipe for disaster.'

Richard Campbell, however, has made a success of it. A keen amateur singer with a passion for travel, he first became involved in organising musical tours as a university student. On graduating, he joined a small student travel company, Sunway Travel, as a tour leader. Thirteen years later, in 1993, he bought the business and repositioned it to focus entirely on musicians, both amateur and professional. It was a successful move and Sunway Travel now arranges worldwide travel for 80% of Britain's classical musicians.

Despite the size of the business, Campbell still enjoys touring with orchestras. 'Musicians are usually delightful to travel with and you visit wonderful places.' It can get stressful though. 'They assume it's normal when everything goes right. If something goes wrong, they look for someone to blame, and they can be quite unreasonable and bad-tempered, especially if they are worried about meeting their contracts for the rest of their tour.'

Campbell explains that things haven't always been easy. 'Sometimes the company didn't perform as well as I'd expected. There were difficult times and I had to learn to cope with the stress. However, we've now got to a level where my staff can run the business on a daily basis and all I need to do is keep an eye on things.'

Campbell recognises that he could have earned more in another line of business. 'Travel generally doesn't pay well. I have friends in other professions who are very highly paid.' But he has no regrets. 'They envy me because I am reasonably well paid to do something that I love doing.'

23 What does Sue Cole say about people whose businesses are their hobbies?

   A   They have the perfect combination.
   B   They risk losing interest in their leisure activity.
   C   They know very little about raising finance.

24 Why do some people who open their own restaurant fail?

   A   They don't learn enough about the competition.
   B   They don't research how to attract customers.
   C   They don't know what turnover levels they need.

25 How did Richard Campbell change Sunway Travel in 1993?

   A   He relocated the company offices.
   B   He targeted a new group of consumers.
   C   He expanded the destinations the company dealt with.

26 According to Campbell, how do musicians react when faced with travel problems?

   A   They try to criticise the person responsible.
   B   They expect things to be put right.
   C   They say they will take their business elsewhere.

27 What does Richard Campbell say about the day-to-day running of his business?

   A   It is unnecessary for him to take an active role.
   B   It has become more stressful.
   C   It is difficult to set realistic targets.

28 What does Richard Campbell feel about his career?

   A   He likes his career though he's always short of money.
   B   He wishes he earned a high salary like his friends.
   C   He's happy and thinks he has enough to live on.

Test 1

PART SIX

Questions 29–40

- Read the job advertisement below.
- Choose the correct word to fill each gap from **A, B** or **C** on the opposite page.
- For each question (**29–40**), mark one letter (**A, B** or **C**) on your Answer Sheet.

Assistant To Public Relations Manager

Business Press is the world's most respected publisher of business news. PR and publicity play (**29**) .... essential part in ensuring our continued (**30**) ...., and this is an outstanding opportunity that (**31**) .... also be the start of a career (**32**) .... Public Relations.

(**33**) .... directly to our PR Manager, you will run her office and learn quickly to do just about everything. Filing documents, taking calls (**34**) .... journalists and answering their questions are all included in (**35**) .... You will also help to organise events and visits, prepare reports (**36**) .... month and generally help to run an efficient press office.

The perfect candidate will have a (**37**) .... standard of education, strong communication skills and an excellent telephone (**38**) .... Professional secretarial qualifications are an advantage. A minimum of two years' experience, (**39**) .... should be within a busy office, is essential. You will be confident, have a smart professional appearance and be in a hurry to '(**40**) .... things done'.

29	A	an	B	each	C	the
30	A	gain	B	success	C	increase
31	A	must	B	ought	C	could
32	A	by	B	with	C	in
33	A	Reporting	B	Reported	C	Report
34	A	for	B	from	C	about
35	A	this	B	them	C	those
36	A	every	B	some	C	any
37	A	deep	B	wide	C	high
38	A	manner	B	attitude	C	approach
39	A	where	B	what	C	which
40	A	make	B	get	C	do

Test 1

PART SEVEN

Questions 41–45

- Read the two memos below.
- Complete the form on the opposite page.
- Write a word or phrase (in CAPITAL LETTERS) or a number on lines **41–45** on your Answer Sheet.

Caradoc Clothing (Manufacturing) Ltd

MEMO

To: Katy Phipps, Personnel Officer
From: Gary Campbell, Design Manager
Date: 19th November 2003
Subject: New vacancy

Sam, the technical assistant in the children's clothes section, has decided to leave on Dec 1st. I'm not sorry, as he had no computer skills. We should insist on that in the ad for a replacement. We usually demand clothes industry experience, but it isn't really necessary – good people can learn very quickly – which means we could use the local paper instead of *Clothing Weekly*. At the moment, we're short of staff in Sportswear, so I want the new person to start there.

Thanks.

Caradoc Clothing (Manufacturing) Ltd

MEMO

To: Jack Thompson, Personnel Advertising
From: Katy Phipps, Personnel Officer
Date: 19th November 2003
Subject: New vacancy

Please note Gary's memo. Sam Cosgrave's leaving on 1 December, so we'd better advertise asap, and aim to get someone from 24 November. Remember the changes to job titles – a technical assistant is now called a design assistant.

28

Staff vacancies

JOB TITLE: (41) ....

STARTING DATE: (42) 2003

SECTION: (43) ....

REQUIREMENT(S): (44) ....

ADVERTISE IN: (45) ....

Test 1

WRITING

PART ONE

Question 46

- You have to cancel a meeting with James Lewis, a senior manager in your company, at very short notice.
- Write an **email** to Mr Lewis:
  - apologising for the cancellation
  - explaining why this was necessary
  - suggesting a date when you are free.
- Write **30–40** words on your Answer Sheet.

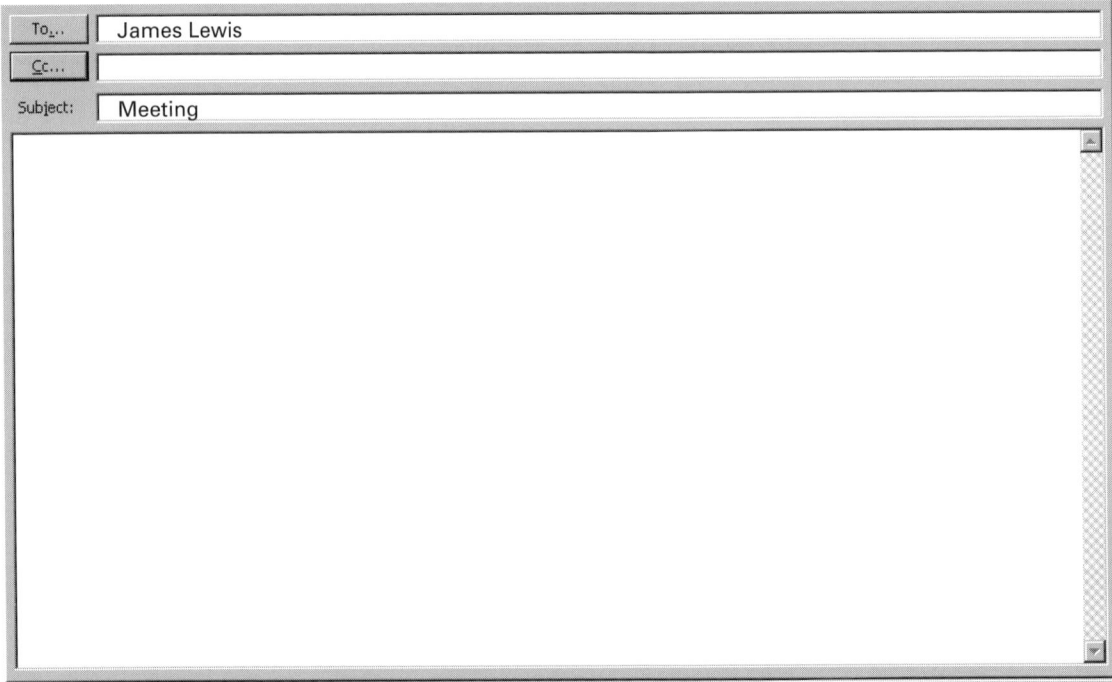

PART TWO

Question 47

- Read part of a letter below from Andrew Trellis inviting you to a business reception at which your company will receive an award.

> We are pleased to inform you that your company has won this year's Business 2003 Award. The award will be presented at a reception at the Park Hotel on February 19.
>
> I would be grateful if you would let me know as soon as you can whether you will be able to attend and, also, whether you would be prepared to give a short talk during the evening.

- Write a **letter** to Mr Trellis:
  - thanking him for the award
  - suggesting a topic for the talk
  - saying what equipment you will need
  - asking whether some members of staff can also attend.
- Write **60–80** words on your Answer Sheet.
- Do not include any postal addresses.

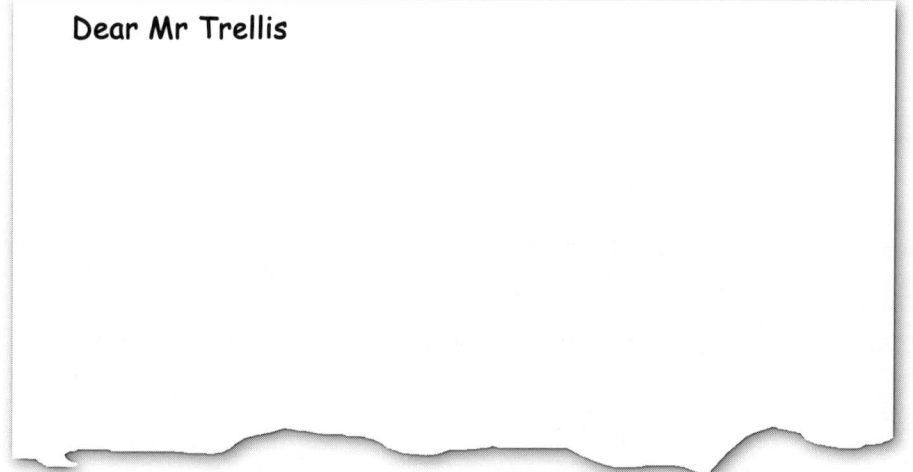

Test 1

LISTENING   Approximately 40 minutes (including 10 minutes' transfer time)

LISTENING

PART ONE   Track 2

Questions 1–8

- For questions **1–8** you will hear eight short recordings.
- For each question, mark **one** letter (**A**, **B** or **C**) for the correct answer.

> **Example:**
>
> Who is Emily going to write to?
>
> **A** the staff
> **B** the supplier
> **C** the clients
>
> The answer is **A**.

Track 3

- After you have listened once, replay each recording.

1   When will the meeting be?

   A   B   C

2   Which office suppliers are they going to use?

Office Network	Excel Products	A-Grade Service
A	B	C

32

Listening

3 Which line shows productivity correctly?

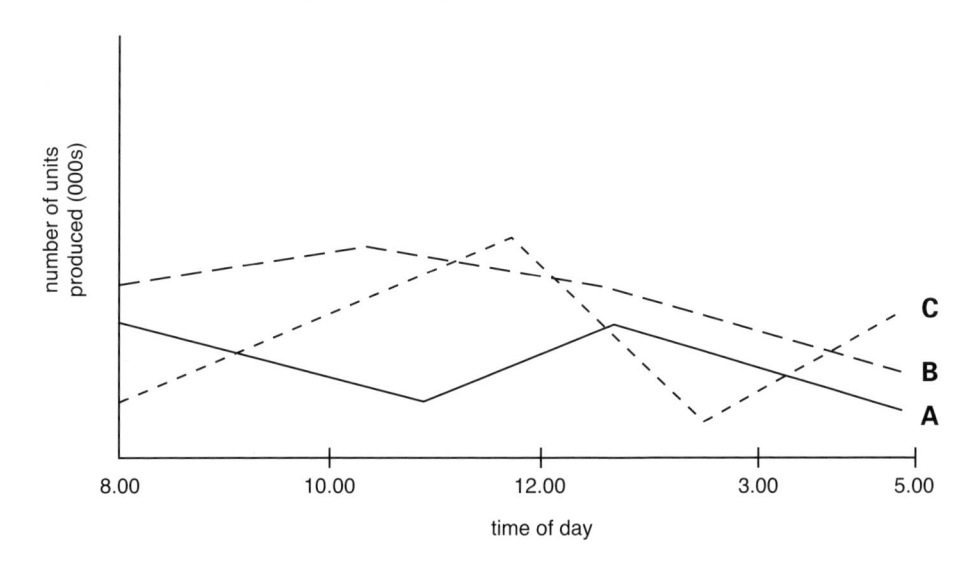

4 What is the correct length?

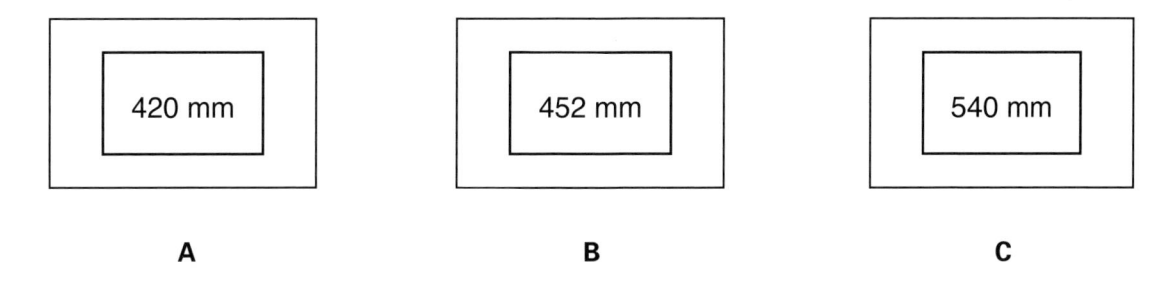

420 mm	452 mm	540 mm
A	B	C

5 What does the woman want to do about the meeting?

    A cancel it
    B postpone it
    C bring it forward

Test 1

6 What time will Mr Johnstone arrive?

14:45	16:50	21:10
A	B	C

7 Which chart shows where the company's goods are made?

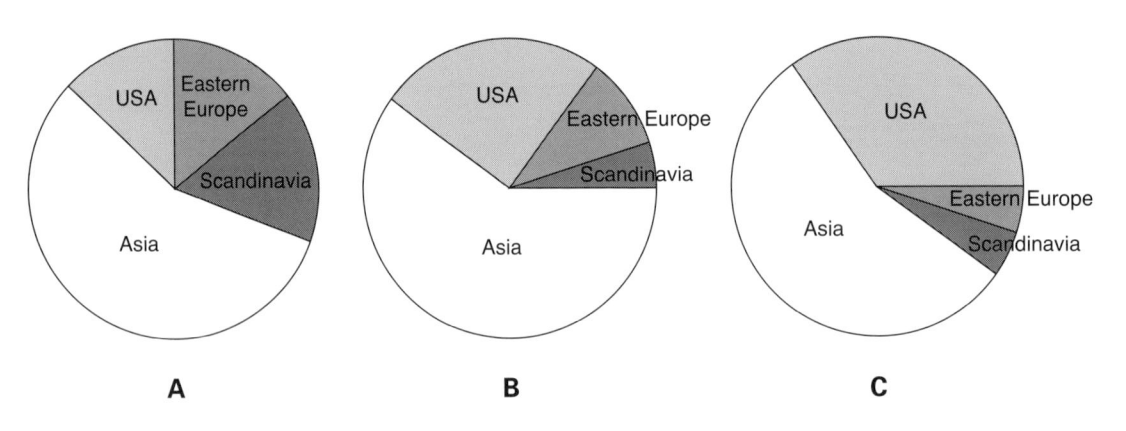

A   B   C

8 Which task is urgent?

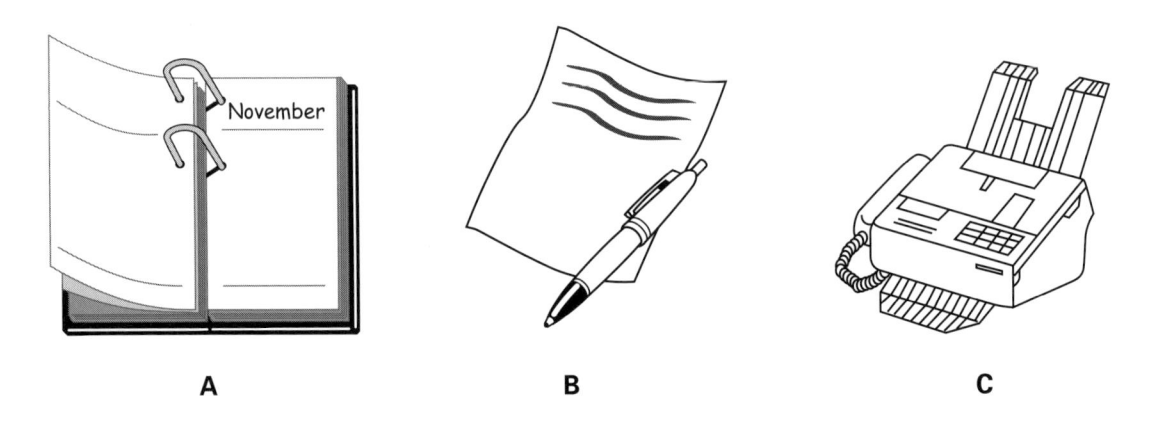

A   B   C

34

Listening

PART TWO

Questions 9–15

- Look at the notes below.
- Some information is missing.
- You will hear an engineering manager giving a secretary some information about a quotation.
- For each question (**9–15**), fill in the missing information in the numbered space using a **word**, **numbers** or **letters**.
- After you have listened once, replay the recording.

Stylex Engineering

Quotation for Service Contract

Customer name: **(9)** .... *International*

Quotation reference: **(10)** ....

Number of machines: **(11)** .... *in packing department*

Charges

Annual service: **(12)** £... *(incl. tax)*

Emergency work

    Call-out charge: **(13)** £...

    New waiting time for call-out: **(14)** .... *hours (guaranteed)*

Payment terms: **(15)** .... *days*

35

PART THREE

Questions 16–22

- Look at the notes about the launch of a new clothing company.
- Some information is missing.
- You will hear part of a welcoming talk by the company's Managing Director.
- For each question (**16–22**), fill in the missing information in the numbered space using **one** or **two** words.
- After you have listened once, replay the recording.

COMPANY LAUNCH EVENT

Notes

New company:

    Name: **(16)** .... Clothing Ltd

Staff change:

    David Shaw to become: **(17)** ....

New premises:

    Location: close to **(18)** ....

    Biggest area of expansion: **(19)** ....

    Future staff facility: **(20)** ....

Future company plans:

    Next new product range: **(21)** .... clothes

    New market: **(22)** ....

Listening

PART FOUR

Questions 23–30

- You will hear a radio interview with George Johnson, Managing Director of Media-X, an organisation which invests in internet companies.
- For each question (**23–30**), mark **one** letter (**A**, **B** or **C**) for the correct answer.
- After you have listened once, replay the recording.

23 The name Media-X was chosen for the company because

    A   it presented a serious image.
    B   it was connected with technology.
    C   it seemed easy to remember.

24 George Johnson started to invest in internet companies because the internet

    A   already had considerable educational value.
    B   was increasingly popular in Europe.
    C   was becoming easier to use.

25 What was George's first job?

    A   bank employee
    B   economics lecturer
    C   software programmer

26 George's father helps him by

    A   advising him on investments.
    B   providing him with suitable office space.
    C   giving him financial support.

27 Approximately how many companies in total does George help each year?

    A   100
    B   200
    C   300

Test 1

28 When choosing between proposals, George first considers

    A the experience of the directors.
    B the need for the product or service.
    C the financial background of the company.

29 Media-X helps companies by providing advice on

    A market research.
    B technical support.
    C pricing strategy.

30 Which of these UK companies has expanded into other countries?

    A NetTrade.com
    B TravelDeals.com
    C OrderFree.com

You now have 10 minutes to transfer your answers to your Answer Sheet.

SPEAKING   12 minutes

SAMPLE SPEAKING TASKS

PART ONE

In this part, the interlocutor asks questions to each of the candidates in turn. You have to give information about yourself and express personal opinions.

PART TWO

In this part of the test, you are asked to give a short talk on a business topic. You have to choose one of the topics from the two below and then talk for about one minute. You have one minute to prepare your ideas.

A: What is important when . . . ?

Choosing a conference centre

- Size of conference centre
- Cost of hiring centre
- Transport connections

B: What is important when . . . ?

Designing a publicity brochure

- Having clear information
- Using pictures
- Giving contact details

PART THREE

In this part of the test, the examiner reads out a scenario and gives you some prompt material in the form of pictures or words. You have 30 seconds to look at the task prompt, an example of which is below, and then about two minutes to discuss the scenario with your partner. After that, the examiner will ask you more questions related to the topic.

For **two** or **three** candidates

Scenario

> I'm going to describe a situation.
>
> **The manufacturing company you work for wants to improve contacts with a local business college. Talk together for about two minutes* about some of the ways the company could help the college and decide which two are best.**
>
> Here are some ideas to help you.

*three minutes for groups of three candidates.

Prompt material

Helping Local Business College

- pay college fees for some students
- provide work experience for students
- give regular presentations at college
- offer jobs to college graduates
- give guided tours of the company
- share sports facilities with the college

Follow-on questions

- Can you think of any other things a company could do to help a local college? (Why?)
- How important do you think practical experience is for business students? (Why?/Why not?)
- What do you think are the advantages to a college of having contacts with local businesses? (Why?/Why not?)
- Do you think there are advantages to a company in having contacts with a local college? (Why?/Why not?)
- Do you think the skills people learn in one company are always useful in another company? (Why?/Why not?)

Test 2

READING AND WRITING   1 hour 30 minutes

READING

PART ONE

Questions 1–5

- Look at questions **1–5**.
- In each question, which sentence is correct?
- For each question, mark one letter (**A**, **B** or **C**) on your Answer Sheet.

Example: 0

> **Telephone message**
> Bill Ryan caught 9.30 flight – due here 11.30 now, not 12.30.

When does Bill Ryan expect to arrive?

A   9.30
B   11.30
C   12.30

The correct answer is **B**, so mark your Answer Sheet like this:

| 0 | A | **B** | C |

1

> Staff wishing to book the firm's social club for private parties must give the manager two weeks' notice.

For private parties, staff should

A   tell the manager in advance.
B   sign the manager's noticeboard.
C   say what kind of event they are planning.

2

> **CUSTOMER HELPLINE**
> Ring us any day, 8.30 am – 5.30 pm.
> First 10 minutes free, then calls charged at local rates.

The cost of calls depends on

A   what time of day it is.
B   how long they last.
C   where the caller lives.

3

> Jane,
>
> Re our new catalogue, just received, Vanters want to see 'Primavera' cloth. Please send samples urgently. (They've got prices.)

Vanters need

A   samples of material.
B   the latest catalogue.
C   a current price list.

4

> WE ARE CURRENTLY RECRUITING TELESALES STAFF.
> EXPERIENCED APPLICANTS SHOULD SUBMIT AN UP-TO-DATE CV
> AND CONTACT DETAILS TO PERSONNEL.

This notice is

A   persuading people to consider starting a career in telesales.
B   instructing staff to give the Personnel department up-to-date paperwork.
C   informing people of the application process for certain vacancies.

5

> **In the event of a fault with this machine, please record the details in the book provided.**

A   To repair the machine, follow the instructions in the book.
B   Consult the book for details before using this machine.
C   If the machine develops a problem, report it in the book.

Test 2

PART TWO

Questions 6–10

- Look at the list below. It shows the contents page from a directory of business services.
- For questions **6–10**, decide which section (**A–H**) of the directory each organisation on the opposite page should consult.
- For each question, mark one letter (**A–H**) on your Answer Sheet.
- Do not use any letter more than once.

BUSINESS SERVICES

A Translation services

B Maps and plans – paper and other media

C Multimedia – electronic publishing

D Music publishing – CDs, audio and video cassettes

E Plastic cards – credit cards, ID cards, etc.

F Business publishing – corporate brochures, documents, etc.

G Design of promotional stickers, labels and signs

H Technical publishing – product manuals, etc.

6 Foresight, a manufacturer of audio equipment, is launching a new range of CD players and needs accompanying instruction booklets.

7 Ream plc, a manufacturer of computer hardware, wants a restyled logo for its new range of laser printers.

8 AFN marketing consultants has prepared a report for a north-African music publisher and requires a version in Arabic.

9 Smart Ltd, a plastic products manufacturer, is planning to produce a high-quality annual report for its shareholders.

10 Stride, a company which makes maps and notices for public places like shopping centres, wants to redesign its website.

PART THREE

Questions 11–15

- Look at the chart below. It shows the domestic sales, foreign sales and profit levels of an electronics manufacturing company over a ten-month period.
- Which month does each sentence (**11–15**) on the opposite page describe?
- For each sentence, mark one letter (**A–H**) on your Answer Sheet.
- Do not use any letter more than once.

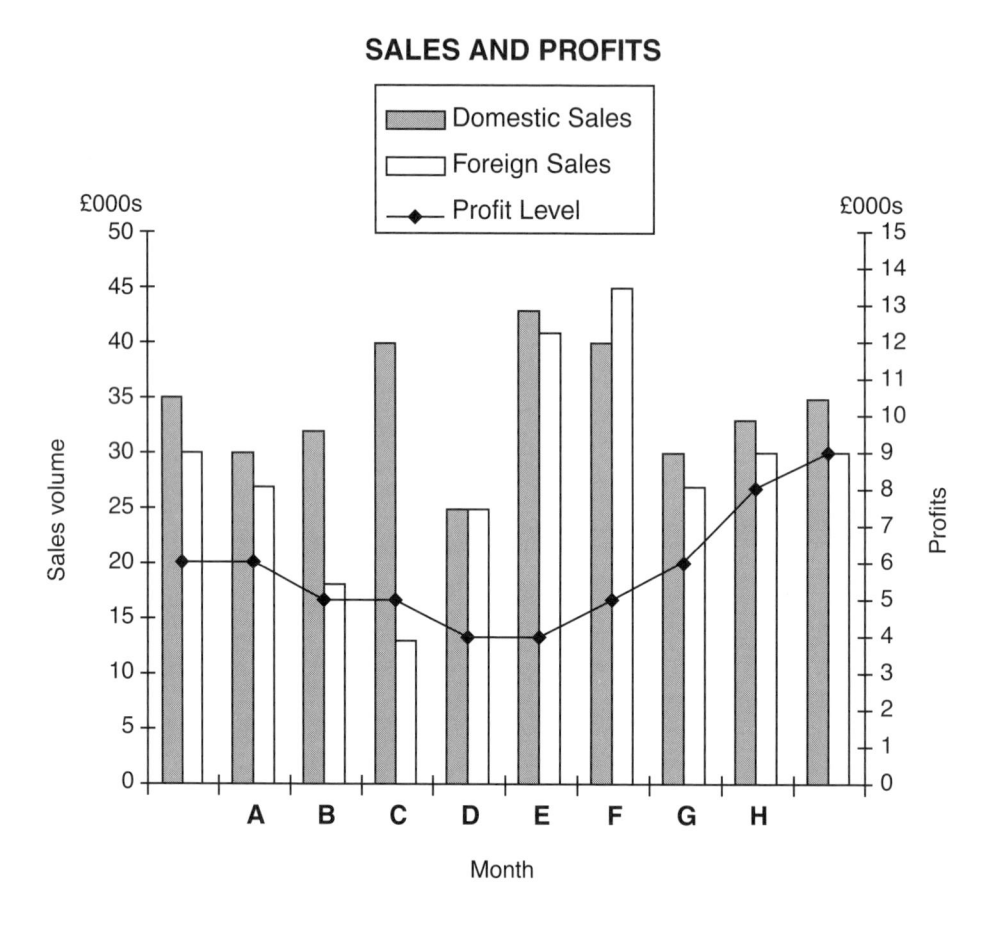

SALES AND PROFITS

11 Although there was a drop in foreign sales, domestic sales continued to rise, which resulted in profit levels holding steady.

12 Domestic sales were higher than foreign sales for the second month running, which boosted profits considerably.

13 While domestic sales rose slightly on the previous month, foreign sales fell, and this led to a slight drop in profits.

14 Despite a downturn in both domestic and foreign sales, profit levels experienced a slight increase.

15 Although domestic sales fell, there was a rise in foreign sales, and this led to a slight increase in profit levels.

PART FOUR

Questions 16–22

- Read the newspaper article below about successful business executives.
- Are sentences **16–22** on the opposite page 'Right' or 'Wrong'? If there is not enough information to answer 'Right' or 'Wrong', choose 'Doesn't say'.
- For each sentence (**16–22**), mark one letter (**A, B** or **C**) on your Answer Sheet.

Why Seeing is Succeeding

Lee Chung of the Seattle Business Institute explains

There are some executives who get it right. They launch winning products, and have a feeling for what customers like and dislike. They do not depend on research or secondary information, and yet they know the market extremely well.

Take Steve Banks, developer of the best-selling personal finance software, Finax. He had noticed how difficult it was to use existing software products, and realised there was a gap in the market. Although 46 competing packages were available when Finax was launched, it quickly succeeded in attracting the majority of customers.

Then consider the UK oil group which learnt that a new chain of hypermarket petrol stations was overtaking its own outlets. The competitor's success was due to a higher standard of service and facilities. The oil group's managers could have discovered this by going to observe these stations for ten minutes. Instead the oil group contacted an agency to carry out more market research.

One of the Institute's most striking findings is that the best business strategists see things for themselves. They do not just analyse, but get out into the field with their customers, and gain first-hand experience of their products.

16 Successful executives base their strategies on reliable data about their clients' requirements.

   A Right   **B** Wrong   **C** Doesn't say

17 Steve Banks made personal contact with product users to discover what they wanted from his software.

   A Right   **B** Wrong   **C** Doesn't say

18 Finax became popular because it was easier to work with than competing products.

   A Right   **B** Wrong   **C** Doesn't say

19 A rival to the UK oil group was performing better because of its pricing policy.

   A Right   **B** Wrong   **C** Doesn't say

20 The UK oil group sent its executives to visit a competitor's petrol stations.

   A Right   **B** Wrong   **C** Doesn't say

21 The UK oil group changed certain policies in order to recover its market share.

   A Right   **B** Wrong   **C** Doesn't say

22 The Seattle Business Institute believes that good business people try out their company's products.

   A Right   **B** Wrong   **C** Doesn't say

PART FIVE

Questions 23–28

- Read the article below about a staff development scheme.
- For each question (**23–28**) on the opposite page, choose the correct answer.
- Mark one letter (**A, B** or **C**) on your Answer Sheet.

Trading Places

Wendy Ledger looks at job swapping, a staff development scheme in which employees exchange jobs for a short period.

According to a recent survey, 77 per cent of people would prefer to work for a boss who offers training and learning in the workplace. One increasingly popular project is job swapping, which gives an insight into the daily challenges facing different people in different roles.

Olivia Yost is a divisional manager with Parker Bridge Ltd, and she recently swapped jobs with the salary controller there. Both were then able to appreciate the problems and pressures of each other's roles far more clearly. Yost says, 'I now have a better understanding of what the salary controller's work involves, and am more aware of my colleague's deadlines. This type of cross training is important, and having to learn about another person's role is a useful experience for bosses and employees alike. Job swapping also helps you to understand the way other departments work and gives you access to other teams within your firm. So it is of value both to the individual and the company as a whole.'

Sean Bradley, who works in central London, took his job exchange a lot further – all the way to Australia in fact. Last July, Sean and his colleague in the Sydney branch of their company swapped jobs. 'I loved it,' said Bradley. 'Primarily for geographic reasons, but also because of the challenge of being the final decision-maker rather than reporting to a manager. It was my first management experience and I had to improve my skills on some IT specialisations. I learnt a lot there, and it was useful too – I've had two promotions since I returned to London.'

Job swapping is an excellent first step towards improving and bringing variety to training and education in the workplace. Doing something else, even for one day, can highlight your abilities and talents, while at the same time drawing attention to any weaknesses. It can also focus the mind on future career possibilities. And even if you hate your time spent at someone else's desk, the worst that can happen is that you'll end up feeling that little bit better about returning to your usual job.

23 According to Olivia Yost, what did she gain from job swapping?

    A   experience of a more stressful working environment
    B   the skills required to gain promotion
    C   an idea of the strict time limits other people face

24 What other advantage of job swapping does Olivia Yost mention?

    A   Companies benefit from having an adaptable workforce.
    B   Staff learn about the overall organisation of their company.
    C   Managers find out which employees are suitable for which jobs.

25 What does Sean Bradley say about working in Australia?

    A   He was surprised at how challenging the job was.
    B   He enjoyed the responsibility which the position involved.
    C   He adapted immediately to the foreign working environment.

26 How did Sean Bradley benefit from his time at the Sydney office?

    A   It taught him valuable communication skills.
    B   It gave him more confidence in his own abilities.
    C   It helped him to progress on his career path.

27 Job swapping raises employees' awareness of

    A   the need to improve certain skills.
    B   the value of effective on-the-job training.
    C   the importance of a flexible approach to work.

28 In some cases, job swapping can make employees

    A   unsure about applying for promotion.
    B   dissatisfied with their present situation.
    C   aware they might be unsuitable for a colleague's job.

Test 2

PART SIX

Questions 29–40

- Read the job advertisement below.
- Choose the correct word to fill each gap from **A**, **B** or **C** on the opposite page.
- For each question (**29–40**), mark one letter (**A, B** or **C**) on your Answer Sheet.

Customer Service Centre Manager Wanted

It's no use providing excellent services if the people they're designed for don't know about them, or aren't sure how to (**29**) .... them. That's why we're opening a Customer Service Centre in July which will provide a model for (**30**) .... more units of this type. The Centre will be on a busy high street so that everyone can see it.

(**31**) .... the manager, you'll be the driving force behind this new venture. To work (**32**) .... this exciting new post, you should have at least two years' management experience in customer services. Your ability to think (**33**) .... and your knowledge of local businesses will (**34**) .... you to plan and run the operations of the Centre to the highest standards and (**35**) .... budget.

(**36**) .... your strong leadership skills, you'll ensure a happy and open environment (**37**) .... all your people can develop, and the service (**38**) .... is always improving.

You will need to communicate well, (**39**) .... with those working in the Centre and external contacts, and you will be required to (**40**) .... excellent presentation and negotiation skills.

29	A	ask	B	require	C	obtain
30	A	many	B	lot	C	few
31	A	As	B	Like	C	Even
32	A	for	B	in	C	by
33	A	ahead	B	through	C	before
34	A	allow	B	let	C	make
35	A	at	B	within	C	during
36	A	Using	B	Use	C	Used
37	A	how	B	when	C	where
38	A	provide	B	provides	C	provided
39	A	each	B	both	C	either
40	A	give	B	supply	C	demonstrate

PART SEVEN

Questions 41–45

- Read the advertisement and the memo below.
- Complete the form on the opposite page.
- Write a word or phrase (in CAPITAL LETTERS) or a number on lines **41–45** on your Answer Sheet.

**THE ELECTRONIC WHITEBOARD
made by Rigley-Turner Limited**

Keep a record of your whiteboard notes without any effort: push a button at the base of the board and a copy is printed out within seconds. The new portable version is lighter than a notebook computer, and fits in the boot of a car.

Type:

Portable size	$985.00
Meeting room size	$870.00
Desk size	$750.00

Only available through the Sales department of your local agent.

Contact: Rightway Supplies
PO Box 2059

Sapient Communications Limited

MEMO

To: Laura Wells
From: Sandra Cooke
Date: 26 March 2004
Subject: Electronic Whiteboard

Laura, these look useful for us in Quality Control. I'd really like the portable, but we'd better ask for the cheapest one. I need it by 10th of next month for the presentation on 15th. Can you fill out a request form in my name and get it to the Purchasing department?

Request Form for Purchase of Equipment

Requested by (full name): **(41)** ....

Department: **(42)** ....

Equipment requested: *Electronic Whiteboard*

    Type: **(43)** ....

Supplier: **(44)** ....

Date required by: **(45)** *2004*

Test 2

WRITING

PART ONE

Question 46

- You would like to attend a sales conference in New York next month, but your department is trying to reduce expenses.
- Write an **email** to your manager, Ross Carpenter:
  - asking him to allow you to go to the conference
  - explaining why you think you should go
  - suggesting how you could reduce the cost of the trip.
- Write **30–40** words on your Answer Sheet.

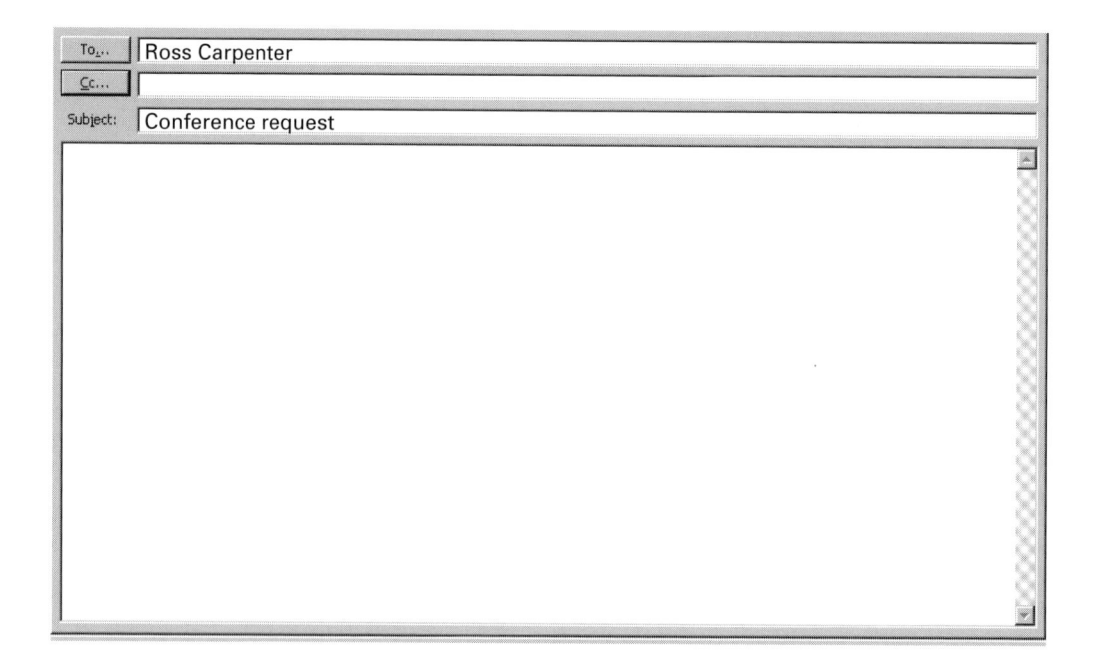

To: Ross Carpenter
Cc:
Subject: Conference request

PART TWO

Question 47

- Read part of a letter below from James French, a local publisher.

> We are preparing a directory of information about businesses in the area. Would it be possible to arrange a convenient time to interview you about your company?
>
> Could you let me know as soon as possible what your company's major activities are, to help in planning the organisation of the directory?

- Write a **letter** to James French:
    - agreeing to his request for an interview
    - giving details of what your company does
    - saying why you would like your company included in the directory
    - asking when the directory will be published.
- Write **60–80** words on your Answer Sheet.
- Do not include any postal addresses.

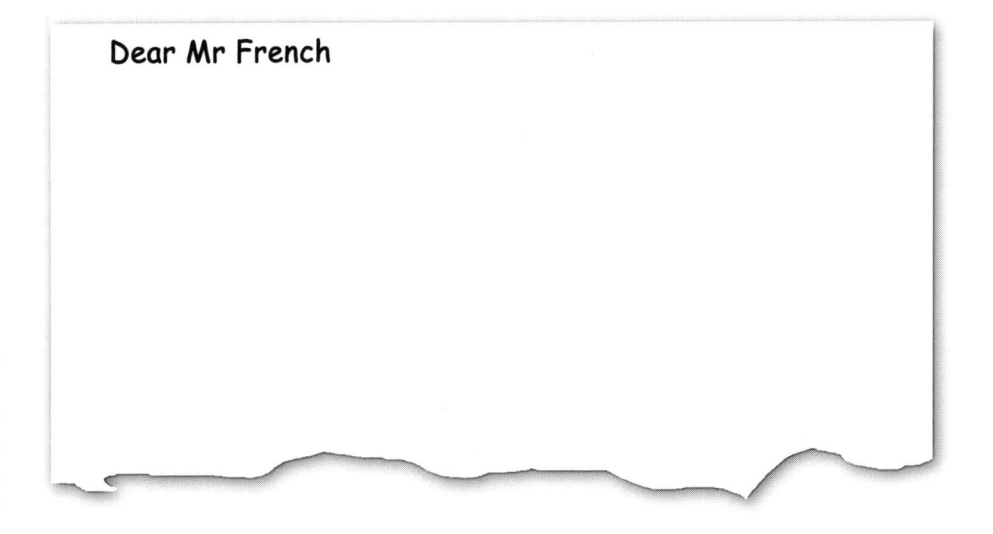

Dear Mr French

Test 2

LISTENING   Approximately 40 minutes (including 10 minutes' transfer time)

LISTENING

PART ONE

Questions 1–8

- For questions **1–8** you will hear eight short recordings.
- For each question, mark **one** letter (**A**, **B** or **C**) for the correct answer.

> **Example:**
>
> Who is Emily going to write to?
>
> **A** the staff
> **B** the supplier
> **C** the clients
>
> The answer is **A**.

- After you have listened once, replay each recording.

1 What interest rate did the man's investment receive this year?

4%	4.5%	5%
A	B	C

2 Which aspect of company policy are staff unhappy about?

A promotion
B salaries
C training

Listening

17 **3** How does the man feel about moving offices?
    A confident
    B anxious
    C disappointed

18 **4** Which graph shows profits at AJB?

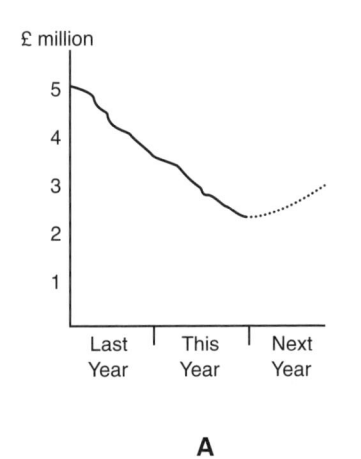

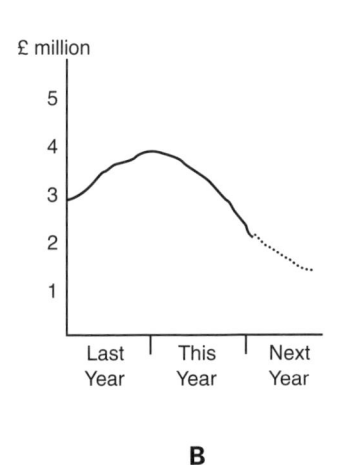

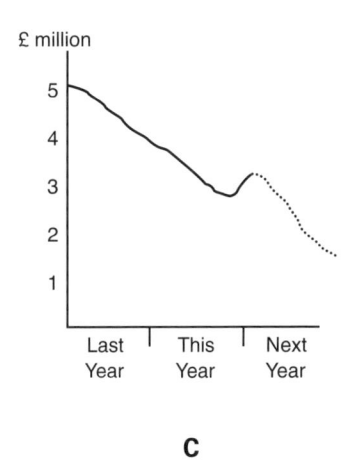

    A   **B**   **C**

19 **5** What percentage of the woman's MBA fees will the company pay?
    A 50%
    B 35%
    C 25%

20 **6** Where is the GNZ Communications stand?

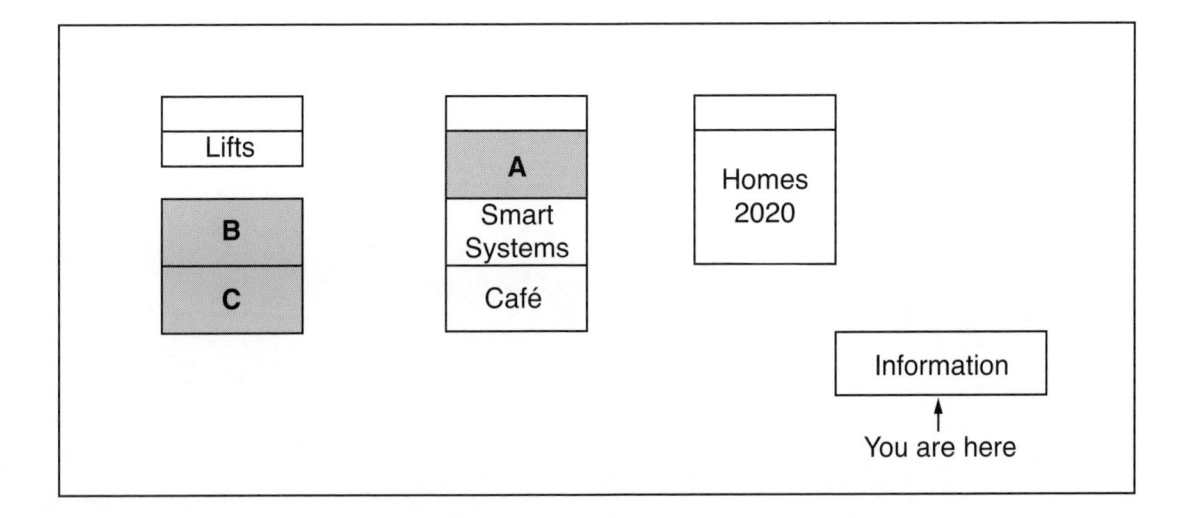

Test 2

7 What time does the man expect to arrive at the meeting?

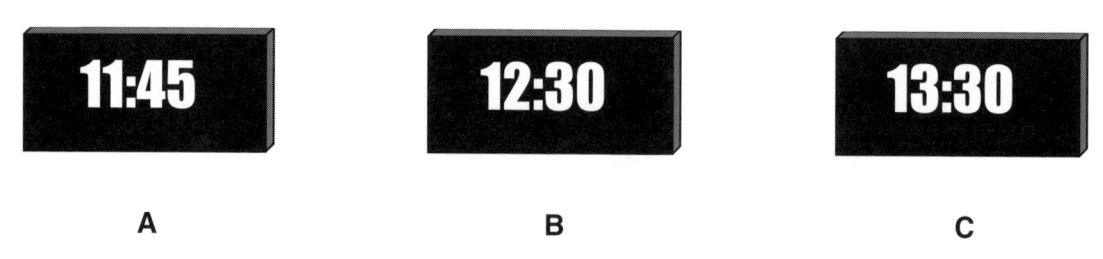

11:45	12:30	13:30
A	**B**	**C**

8 Which chart shows the company's current income by country?

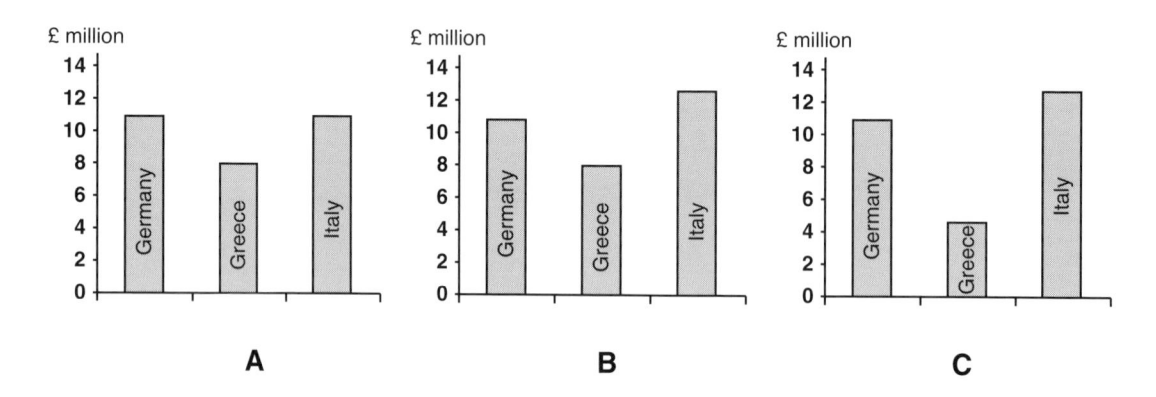

A, B, C: bar charts showing £ million by Germany, Greece, Italy.

- **A**: Germany ~11, Greece ~8, Italy ~11
- **B**: Germany ~11, Greece ~8, Italy ~12.5
- **C**: Germany ~11, Greece ~4.5, Italy ~12.5

Listening

PART TWO

Questions 9–15 Track 23

- Look at the notes below.
- Some information is missing.
- You will hear a man giving some information about a conference.
- For each question (**9–15**), fill in the missing information in the numbered space using a **word**, **numbers** or **letters**.
- After you have listened once, replay the recording.

GLOBALNET CONFERENCE 2004

Contact name:		*Tim Adams*
Conference starts on:	(9)	.... *November*
Venue:	(10)	.... *Conference Centre*
Number of exhibitors:	(11)	....
Name of first speaker:	(12)	*Mike* ....
Seminars begin at:	(13)	....
Advance ticket cost:	(14)	£ ....
Ticket reservation telephone number:	(15)	....

61

Test 2

PART THREE

Questions 16–22 Track 24

- Look at the notes about the career of Steven Jackson.
- Some information is missing.
- You will hear part of a presentation given by Steven Jackson at an interview.
- For each question (**16–22**), fill in the missing information in the numbered space using **one** or **two** words.
- After you have listened once, replay the recording.

Interview notes – career of Steven Jackson

Current position:	(16) ....
Company's main product:	(17) ....
Company name:	(18) ....
Subject studied at university:	(19) ....
Previous job:	(20) ....
Languages spoken other than English:	(21) .... and ....
Can start in:	(22) ....

Listening

PART FOUR Track 25

Questions 23–30

- You will hear a discussion between James, the General Manager, and Sarah, the Office Manager, of a company.
- For each question (**23–30**), mark **one** letter (**A**, **B** or **C**) for the correct answer.
- After you have listened once, replay the recording.

23 What is James most interested in discussing?

    A   computer systems
    B   staff performance
    C   flexible working hours

24 James says that Peter Jones has produced

    A   his reports late.
    B   only one report.
    C   very short reports.

25 James and Sarah discuss organising a workshop on

    A   team building.
    B   cost cutting.
    C   time management.

26 In March, the company is going to

    A   install new computer software.
    B   start using new computer software.
    C   test the new computer software.

27 Where will staff do the computer course?

    A   at the training centre
    B   on site
    C   in the college

Test 2

28 The Accounts department will move to the

    A first floor.
    B second floor.
    C third floor.

29 According to Sarah, there are still problems in the Accounts department with

    A the fax machine.
    B the printers.
    C the photocopier.

30 What will James and Sarah discuss at their next meeting?

    A the Health and Safety report
    B the programme for the French clients
    C the appointment of a new PA

You now have 10 minutes to transfer your answers to your Answer Sheet.

SPEAKING   12 minutes

SAMPLE SPEAKING TASKS

PART ONE

In this part, the interlocutor asks questions to each of the candidates in turn. You have to give information about yourself and express personal opinions.

PART TWO

In this part of the test, you are asked to give a short talk on a business topic. You have to choose one of the topics from the two below and then talk for about one minute. You have one minute to prepare your ideas.

A: What is important when . . . ?

Considering a job in another country

- Length of contract
- Financial advantages of the job
- Availability of language training

B: What is important when . . . ?

Choosing an employee for promotion

- Length of service
- Motivation
- Performance

Test 2

PART THREE

In this part of the test, the examiner reads out a scenario and gives you some prompt material in the form of pictures or words. You have 30 seconds to look at the task prompt, an example of which is below, and then about two minutes to discuss the scenario with your partner. After that, the examiner will ask you more questions related to the topic.

For **two** or **three** candidates

Scenario

> I'm going to describe a situation.
>
> **The company you work for is going to send one employee to an English-speaking country for one month on a sales trip. Talk together for about two minutes* about three of the employees and decide which one would be best.**
>
> Here are some ideas to help you.

*three minutes for groups of three candidates.

Prompt material

Foreign Sales Trip			
	Mrs Da Silva	**Mr Perez**	**Ms Yamada**
Time with company:	25 years	14 years	1 year
Foreign Languages:	good English, Spanish and German	good English and French	good English and basic Korean
Sales Experience:	15 years at home and overseas	10 years in home market	2 sales trips abroad
Personal Qualities:	not very confident when working alone	good team leader	excellent communication skills

Follow-on questions

- How important do you think it is to speak the language of the people you are selling to? (Why?/Why not?)

- What special qualities do you think a good sales person needs? (Why?/Why not?)

- Do you think it's better to send one person or a team of people on a sales trip? (Why?/Why not?)

- Do you think sales people should be allowed to take their families with them on foreign trips? (Why?/Why not?)

- What problems do you think there could be when selling products in another country? (Why?/Why not?)

Test 3

READING AND WRITING 1 hour 30 minutes

READING

PART ONE

Questions 1–5

- Look at questions **1–5**.
- In each question, which sentence is correct?
- For each question, mark one letter (**A**, **B** or **C**) on your Answer Sheet.

Example: 0

Telephone message

Bill Ryan caught 9.30 flight – due here 11.30 now, not 12.30.

When does Bill Ryan expect to arrive?

A 9.30
B 11.30
C 12.30

The correct answer is **B**, so mark your Answer Sheet like this:

| 0 | A | B | C |

1

PLEASE NOTE THAT, DUE TO HIGHER FUEL COSTS, CHARGES FOR OUR EXPRESS DELIVERY SERVICE HAVE NOW INCREASED.

This service will cost more because

A petrol prices have risen.
B the delivery of goods is taking longer.
C vehicles are more expensive to buy.

2

Secretaries – looking for work?
Email your CV to us now! Include details of required salary.

Click here

- **A** Email your details to us, mentioning what salary you want.
- **B** For secretarial staff, email us, stating what salary you pay.
- **C** Email us for an application form, saying what your salary is.

3

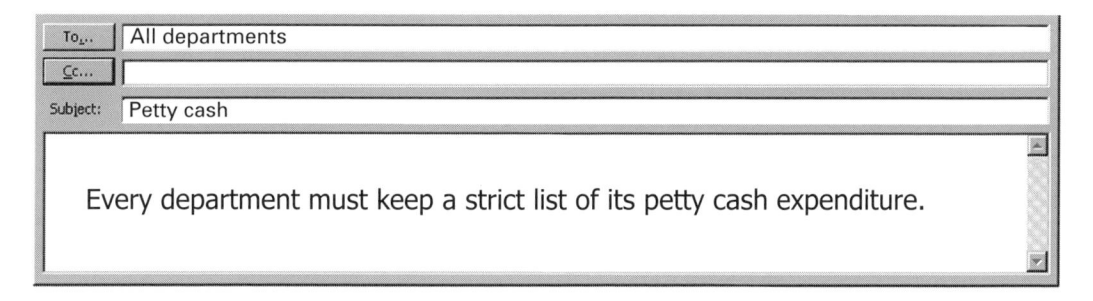

To... All departments
Cc...
Subject: Petty cash

Every department must keep a strict list of its petty cash expenditure.

Every department is required to

- **A** spend money only on items in the list.
- **B** keep to the spending limit given in the list.
- **C** list all the money it spends on miscellaneous items.

4

ANNIVERSARY EVENT: 6 AUGUST

Brickworks Ltd invites employees and their families to an evening entertainment in Weston Park.

- **A** Brickworks Ltd is celebrating its sixth anniversary in Weston Park.
- **B** Employees will entertain Brickworks' guests in Weston Park in August.
- **C** Staff can take their families to Brickworks' evening entertainment.

5

CONFERENCE RECEPTION

Delegates can collect pre-paid passes from here.
Passes may be purchased at event organiser's office.

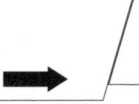

Delegates should go to reception if

- **A** they bought passes before the conference.
- **B** they have already collected their pass.
- **C** they want to purchase conference passes.

Test 3

PART TWO

Questions 6–10

- Look at the list below. It shows the business-to-business services offered by a consultancy group.
- For questions **6–10**, decide which service (**A–H**) each person on the opposite page needs.
- For each question, mark one letter (**A–H**) on your Answer Sheet.
- Do not use any letter more than once.

PUCKERIDGE CONSULTANCY GROUP

We offer the following services:

A   vehicles and drivers for all goods/routes

B   advice on legal requirements for imports/exports

C   staff pay records produced for all company types

D   electronic files adapted for most software programmes

E   software for predicting sales

F   container units for hire

G   effective recruitment advertising

H   workplace skills training

6 Kenichi Saitoshi runs an expanding law firm, and needs help with filling vacant posts.

7 Manfred Wirsing is a divisional manager who wants to set appropriate production targets for the coming year.

8 Jennifer Lee's manufacturing company has purchased material from overseas, and is looking for a suitable place to keep it.

9 John Black's packaging company wants to be able to send customers in other countries invoices and receipts online.

10 Asma Samairat wants staff at her transport company to improve their keyboard accuracy.

Test 3

PART THREE

Questions 11–15

- Look at the charts below. They show the sales of eight companies' two top-selling products over a three-year period.
- Which chart does each sentence (**11–15**) on the opposite page describe?
- For each sentence, mark one letter (**A–H**) on your Answer Sheet.
- Do not use any letter more than once.

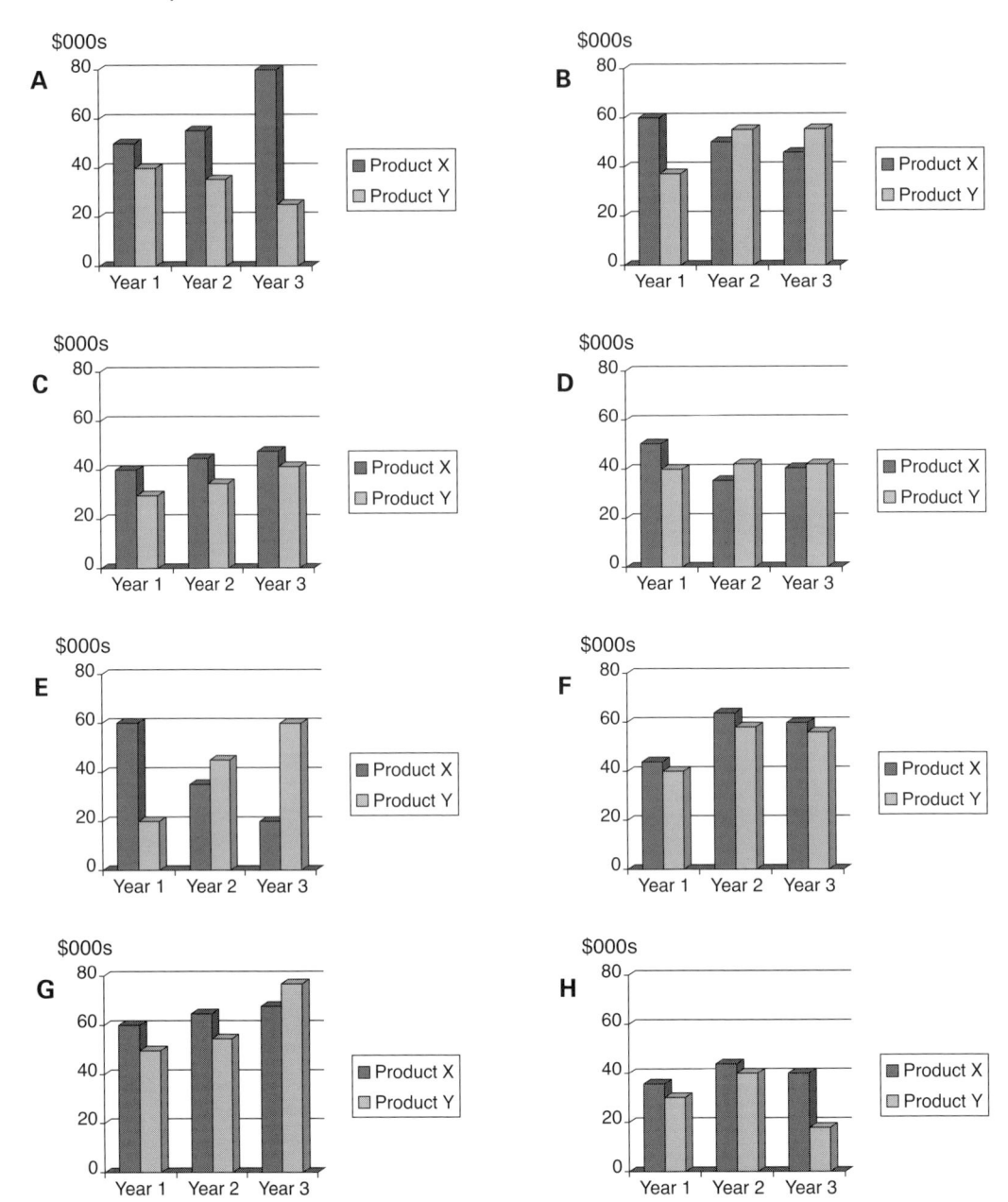

11 Sales of both products increased in year 2, then fell back slightly, while staying above their original levels.

12 Both products saw their sales climb steadily during the period, product X remaining ahead of product Y.

13 Product Y's sales overtook those of product X in year 2, then remained steady as product X's recovered.

14 An improvement in both products' sales in year 2 was followed by a drop, which was greater for product Y.

15 The gap between sales figures for product X and product Y increased year on year, with product Y always selling less than product X.

Test 3

PART FOUR

Questions 16–22

- Read the article below about working in different sized companies.
- Are sentences **16–22** on the opposite page 'Right' or 'Wrong'? If there is not enough information to answer 'Right' or 'Wrong', choose 'Doesn't say'.
- For each sentence (**16–22**), mark one letter (**A**, **B** or **C**) on your Answer Sheet.

Choose your company with care

Small is beautiful. That, at least, is the conclusion of new research examining how satisfied secretaries are in different sized firms. 'We have found that people who work for small or medium-sized companies work harder and are more committed,' says David Smith, author of one of the latest studies in this field. 'The smaller the environment, the bigger the part you play as an individual, and the more people notice your absence.'

This will come as a surprise to many secretaries. Some recruitment agencies said that secretaries are keen to get positions in the bigger companies.

However, smaller companies can be more flexible when it comes to working hours, and have better working conditions. But working for a smaller firm is not without its disadvantages. Career development in the form of courses can be limited, but, on the other hand, employees often feel that they can learn more on the job.

In fact, opportunities for promotion are the same whatever the size of the company. Smith also says: 'Our research shows that in a company of fewer than 50 people, employers can actually see what their employees are producing and then give them bonuses as appropriate.'

16 The new research focuses on the number of secretaries employed in small firms.

    A Right   **B** Wrong   **C** Doesn't say

17 Medium-sized companies pay their secretaries more than small companies do.

    A Right   **B** Wrong   **C** Doesn't say

18 Secretaries in smaller firms are more important to the organisation than the ones in larger firms.

    A Right   **B** Wrong   **C** Doesn't say

19 Agencies sometimes find that secretaries prefer to work for larger organisations.

    A Right   **B** Wrong   **C** Doesn't say

20 Large companies regularly run their own courses for secretaries.

    A Right   **B** Wrong   **C** Doesn't say

21 Large companies promote secretaries more often than small companies do.

    A Right   **B** Wrong   **C** Doesn't say

22 Bosses in small companies reward secretaries financially if they are pleased with their work.

    A Right   **B** Wrong   **C** Doesn't say

PART FIVE

Questions 23–28

- Read the article below about an insurance company.
- For each question (**23–28**) on the opposite page, choose the correct answer.
- Mark one letter (**A, B** or **C**) on your Answer Sheet.

Success Story

Journalist Mark Stretton examines the growth of an insurance company which now has sales of £300 million per year.

In 1993, American-born Henry Eastman got a call from a recruitment consultancy, inviting him to give up his successful marketing career in one insurance company to become the head of another. This new job was to work for an investment company called Brinscombe's, who wanted him to create a brand new car insurance company. Despite the risks involved, Eastman agreed.

A lot of young drivers in the 20 to 35 age range, especially the ones who have already had accidents, have difficulties in getting car insurance because most companies think they are too big a risk. However, Eastman believes there are no problems if their annual payments are large enough. He offered them insurance cover through television commercials and attracted many customers by giving out folders in which to keep their policies safe. His strategy was a good one. Within eight years he had built the business into a national company with 500,000 customers and sales of £300 million per year.

The company is based in Manchester. The authorities there wanted to increase employment and offered Eastman a £1 million grant to start up after he promised to create 350 new jobs. He is now a major employer in the area with 1,400 staff and has also created new specialist insurance companies for women, credit card users and people using the internet.

Eastman believes in American management methods: working as a team to get better results; not being allowed to miss lunch because you are too busy; and having fun. This belief has recently won him a place in a '50 Best Companies to Work For' survey.

In 1999, Brinscombe's decided to withdraw their investment and offered the company to the management team. They said 'yes', borrowed £80 million from a bank and bought it. Eastman is pleased with his success. 'We're a great and growing company', he says, 'and we give our customers better service than they can dream of!'

23 Henry Eastman's previous job was in

   A   recruitment.
   B   marketing.
   C   investment.

24 He was offered the opportunity to

   A   take over a company called Brinscombe's.
   B   invest his own money in a new company.
   C   set up a company for someone else.

25 The company's success is due to

   A   refusing insurance to high-risk clients.
   B   selling cheap insurance policies.
   C   targeting a particular market.

26 He chose the present company location because

   A   financial support was available in that part of the country.
   B   it would be easy to expand the premises.
   C   there was already a skilled workforce.

27 Eastman's strategy is to

   A   produce a happy working environment.
   B   encourage staff to decide on their own objectives.
   C   make each person work as hard as possible.

28 The company is now owned by

   A   Brinscombe's.
   B   Eastman and his colleagues.
   C   a co-operative of customers.

PART SIX

Questions 29–40

- Read the minutes below from a Health and Safety committee meeting.
- Choose the correct word to fill each gap from **A**, **B** or **C** on the opposite page.
- For each question (**29–40**), mark one letter (**A**, **B** or **C**) on your Answer Sheet.

Minutes

Lighting

Staff are complaining about the poor lighting in the main office. The secretary of the committee recently obtained quotes (**29**) .... new lighting, (**30**) .... we passed to the management board. The committee is (**31**) .... waiting for (**32**) .... decision. We are hoping the board will let us (**33**) .... within the next few weeks.

New Drinks Machine

Of the three types of machine we looked at, Maxcup appeared to be the best option. The committee now has to find a new (**34**) ...., as our current machine causes problems near the fire exit (**35**) .... several people use the machine at the same time. It was decided to put (**36**) .... taking the decision, and we expect to have enough information (**37**) .... the end of the month.

Conference Attendance

John (**38**) .... to be away at the conference from 1st to 8th of next month. Rebecca has agreed to assist us in his (**39**) .... John has a useful list of contacts in (**40**) .... to help her research new safety equipment.

Next committee meeting: 16th March.

29	**A** from	**B** for	**C** of
30	**A** what	**B** when	**C** which
31	**A** still	**B** yet	**C** already
32	**A** your	**B** our	**C** their
33	**A** known	**B** knowing	**C** know
34	**A** location	**B** size	**C** design
35	**A** whether	**B** unless	**C** if
36	**A** through	**B** off	**C** up
37	**A** by	**B** until	**C** on
38	**A** believes	**B** thinks	**C** expects
39	**A** leave	**B** absence	**C** departure
40	**A** time	**B** order	**C** case

PART SEVEN

Questions 41–45

- Read the memo and the advertisement below.
- Complete the form on the opposite page.
- Write a word or phrase (in CAPITAL LETTERS) or a number on lines **41–45** on your Answer Sheet.

King's Human Resources Consultancy

MEMO

To: Jim White/PA
From: Marjory King/Director
Date: 22/5/04
Subject: Conference

We're taking part in the HR conference again. Gillian Rolland has agreed to give a talk on international recruitment, and she'll take three colleagues along with her. Except for Mark Hughes, they'll require single rooms for the evening before. Gillian would rather attend the earlier conference – she's busy the week after. She's giving a Powerpoint presentation and just needs a screen – she'll take her laptop with her. Please make the booking asap.

HUMAN RESOURCES CONFERENCE 2004

There will be two one-day conferences this year – one in Edinburgh on September 2 and one in London on September 12.

The booking fee is £400 per company, payable four weeks in advance. For groups of five or more, the fee (with a 20% reduction) is £320.

Please complete the attached form and send to Simon Winters.

CONFERENCE BOOKING FORM: REGISTRATION DETAILS

Preferred location: (41) ....

Number of delegates: 4

Number of hotel rooms required: (42) .... *single rooms*

Guest speaker (full name): (43) ....

Equipment required: (44) ....

Fee payable: (45) £ ....

Test 3

WRITING

PART ONE

Question 46

- You plan to attend a seminar next week and you think your colleague Liz will also be interested in going.
- Write a **note** to your colleague, Liz:
  - telling her what the seminar is about
  - explaining why you think it would help in her work
  - suggesting that you travel to the seminar together.
- Write **30–40** words on your Answer Sheet.

Liz,

PART TWO

Question 47

- Read part of a fax below from Gerald Davis, a colleague in the London office of your company.

> As you know, we regularly use the Station Hotel in London for business meetings. However, some clients have recently complained about the business facilities at the hotel. We would be grateful if you could give us your opinion.
>
> For your next visit on 28th August, would you prefer to stay there or at another hotel? In addition, would you like us to arrange a company car from the airport?

- Write a **fax** to Gerald Davis:
  - giving your opinion of the Station Hotel
  - comparing its business facilities with another hotel
  - saying which hotel you would prefer in August
  - accepting the company car.
- Write **60–80** words on your Answer Sheet.
- Do not include any postal addresses.

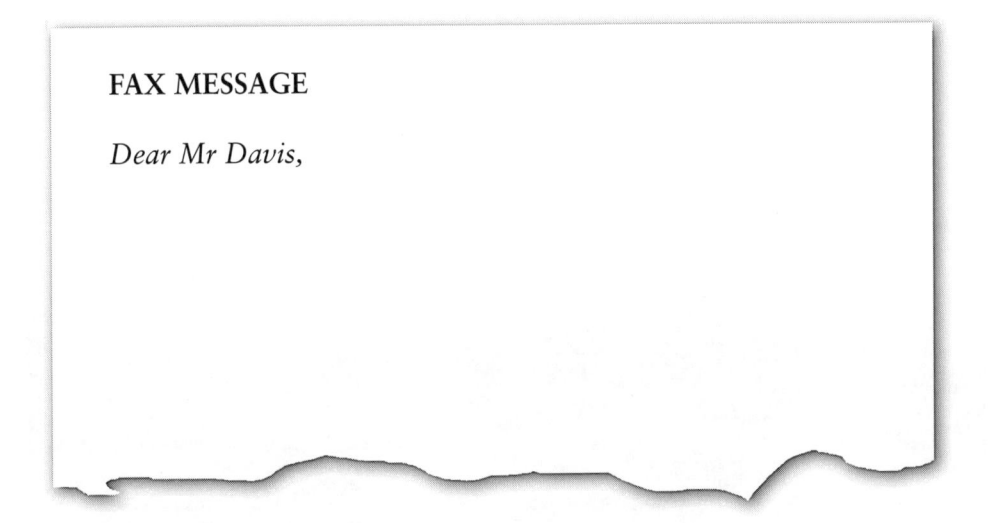

FAX MESSAGE

Dear Mr Davis,

Test 3

LISTENING Approximately 40 minutes (including 10 minutes' transfer time)

LISTENING

PART ONE

Questions 1–8

- For questions **1–8** you will hear eight short recordings.
- For each question, mark **one** letter (**A**, **B** or **C**) for the correct answer.

> **Example:**
>
> Who is Emily going to write to?
>
> **A** the staff
> **B** the supplier
> **C** the clients
>
> The answer is **A**.

- After you have listened once, replay each recording.

1 What does George think about the new company magazine?

   A It is a useful resource.
   B It costs too much to produce.
   C It looks boring.

2 In which product range are sales growing most quickly?

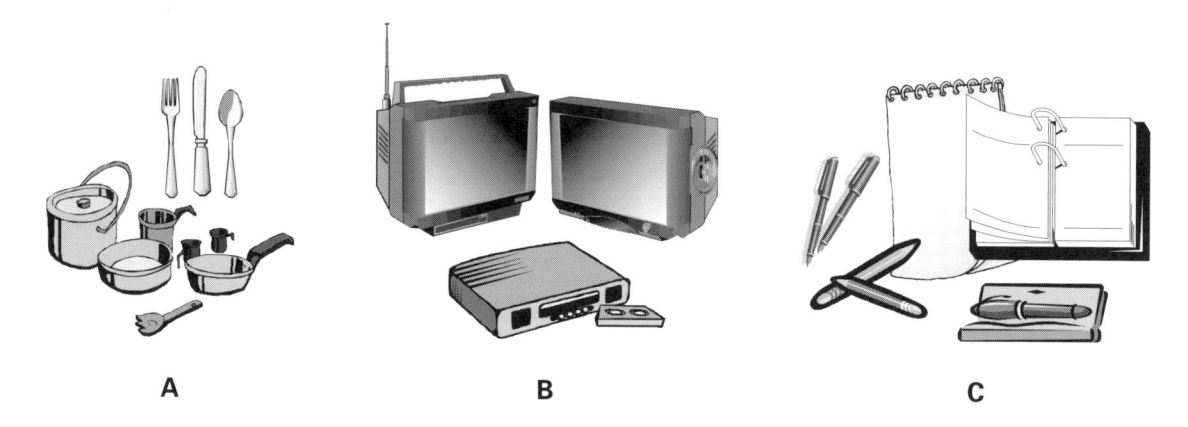

A   B   C

84

Listening

3   Which set of information is unavailable?

    A   information about sales staff
    B   information about products
    C   information about stores

4   Where is the Human Resources department?

```
┌─────────────────────────────────────────────────────────────┐
│                        CORRIDOR                             │
│─────────────────┬──────────────────────┬────────────────────│
│ HUMAN RESOURCES │      MARKETING       │        LIFT        │
└─────────────────┴──────────────────────┴────────────────────┘
                               A
```

```
┌─────────────────────────────────────────────────────────────┐
│                        CORRIDOR                             │
│─────────────────┬──────────────────────┬────────────────────│
│    MARKETING    │   HUMAN RESOURCES    │        LIFT        │
└─────────────────┴──────────────────────┴────────────────────┘
                               B
```

```
┌─────────────────────────────────────────────────────────────┐
│                        CORRIDOR                             │
│─────────┬──────────────────────┬────────────────────────────│
│  LIFT   │      MARKETING       │      HUMAN RESOURCES       │
└─────────┴──────────────────────┴────────────────────────────┘
                               C
```

5   Which hotel are they going to book for Mr Sands?

    A   The Crown
    B   The Laurel
    C   The Westgate

Test 3

6 Why is the man phoning?

    A to make an appointment
    B to cancel an appointment
    C to postpone an appointment

7 How much does the man earn in total at the moment?

    A £35,000
    B £40,000
    C £46,000

8 Which graph shows the company's future sales targets?

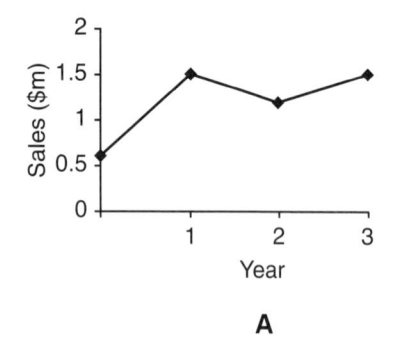

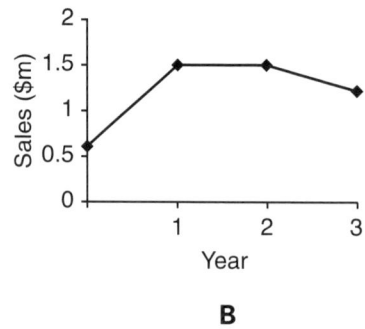

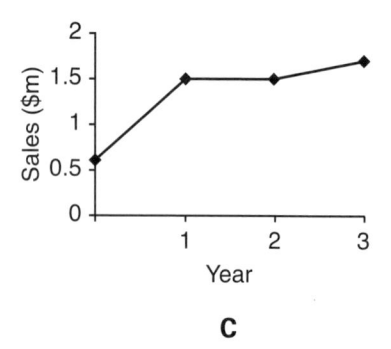

    A   **B**   **C**

Listening

PART TWO

Questions 9–15

- Look at the form below.
- Some information is missing.
- You will hear a man phoning the Human Resources department of the company where he works.
- For each question (**9–15**), fill in the missing information in the numbered space using a **word**, **numbers** or **letters**.
- After you have listened once, replay the recording.

New member of staff – details

Name:	**(9)**	Ms ....
Starting date:	**(10)**	....
Phone extension:	**(11)**	....
Email address:	**(12)**	.... @horsham.com
Network password:	**(13)**	....
Starting salary:	**(14)**	£ ....
Home address:	**(15)**	.... West Street, Kenford

Test 3

PART THREE

Questions 16–22

- Look at the notes about a designer.
- Some information is missing.
- You will hear part of a speech by a designer who is accepting an award.
- For each question (**16–22**), fill in the missing information in the numbered space using **one** or **two** words.
- After you have listened once, replay the recording.

UK Design Award – notes on winning designer

First worked in a	(16) ....
1989: Became senior manager of a	(17) .... chain
Country where first successful exhibition was held:	(18) ....
2003: Awarded Conrad Prize for the	(19) .... programme
Would like to thank his	(20) ....

Recent developments:

Won contract with Swedish firm to design new range of	(21) ....
New partner called:	(22) ....

PART FOUR

Questions 23–30

- You will hear Janet Willis, a management consultant, advising David Smith, a managing director, about using a marketing services agency.
- For each question (**23–30**), mark **one** letter (**A**, **B** or **C**) for the correct answer.
- After you have listened once, replay the recording.

23 Why does Janet Willis think they need to use an outside agency?

    A   because the business is growing quickly
    B   because the business is not growing fast enough
    C   because the business is falling behind its competitors

24 Janet thinks the main advantage of using an agency would be

    A   to advise on recruitment.
    B   to provide staff training.
    C   to save the company time.

25 Which agency does she recommend?

    A   Walker Taylor
    B   Duffy & Partners
    C   Red Ribbon

26 How does she think the company should use the agency?

    A   to audit their marketing plans
    B   to work with them as a long-term partner
    C   to help with the next product launch

27 When negotiating the contract, she recommends

    A   having limited objectives.
    B   being able to choose the agency staff.
    C   insisting on payment by results.

28 Janet thinks the key to a successful client/agency relationship is

    A complete trust.
    B close control.
    C frequent meetings.

29 Janet thinks the main cause for this relationship breaking down is

    A lack of staff involvement.
    B lack of communication.
    C lack of positive decision-making.

30 By the end of the conversation, the MD

    A is still not sure he wants to use an agency.
    B is enthusiastic about using an agency.
    C has decided against using an agency.

You now have 10 minutes to transfer your answers to your Answer Sheet.

SPEAKING   12 minutes

SAMPLE SPEAKING TASKS

PART ONE

In this part, the interlocutor asks questions to each of the candidates in turn. You have to give information about yourself and express personal opinions.

PART TWO

In this part of the test, you are asked to give a short talk on a business topic. You have to choose one of the topics from the two below and then talk for about one minute. You have one minute to prepare your ideas.

A: What is important when . . . ?

Promoting a new product

- Cost of product
- Advertising
- Free samples

B: What is important when . . . ?

Working in a team

- Deciding people's responsibilities
- Sharing information
- Having a team leader

Test 3

PART THREE

In this part of the test, the examiner reads out a scenario and gives you some prompt material in the form of pictures or words. You have 30 seconds to look at the task prompt, an example of which is below, and then about two minutes to discuss the scenario with your partner. After that, the examiner will ask you more questions related to the topic.

For **two** or **three** candidates

Scenario

> I'm going to describe a situation.
>
> **The company you work for has invited a group of business students to spend a day at the premises. Talk together for about two minutes* about some of the things the company could arrange for the students and decide which three would be most useful.**
>
> Here are some ideas to help you.

*three minutes for groups of three candidates.

Prompt material

Visit by Business Students
- Tour of administration offices
- Visit to IT department
- Lunch with Personnel Manager
- Tour of staff facilities
- Visit to Production department
- Meetings with individual employees

Follow-on questions

- Would you like to take a group of student visitors on a tour of your company? (Why?/Why not?)
- What kinds of information about a company would not be suitable for a group of student visitors? (Why?)
- What are the advantages to companies of inviting business students to visit their offices? (Why?)
- What other things can companies do to help business students in their training? (Why?)
- What kinds of support can companies give to the area where they are located? (Why?)

Test 4

READING AND WRITING   1 hour 30 minutes

READING

PART ONE

Questions 1–5

- Look at questions **1–5**.
- In each question, which sentence is correct?
- For each question, mark one letter (**A**, **B** or **C**) on your Answer Sheet.

Example: 0

Telephone message

Bill Ryan caught 9.30 flight – due here 11.30 now, not 12.30.

When does Bill Ryan expect to arrive?

A   9.30
B   11.30
C   12.30

The correct answer is **B**, so mark your Answer Sheet like this:

| 0 | A | B | C |

1

Payment for overtime is made monthly but claim forms cannot be processed unless they are authorised by supervisors.

A   Payments for overtime are made at the end of the month.
B   Applications to do overtime must be signed by supervisors.
C   Claims for overtime should be approved by supervisors.

2

Select any three products and obtain the cheapest one free.
Applies only to full price items.

A   Customers buying three products will only pay for the most expensive two.
B   Customers who pay for three products will receive a fourth free.
C   Customers can only choose the free product from discounted goods.

3

> Marc,
>
> This is a sample of the proposed business card. Your comments on the layout would be appreciated.

What should Marc do?

- **A** select one of the designs for the business card
- **B** give an opinion on the design of the business card
- **C** check the changes to the business card design

4

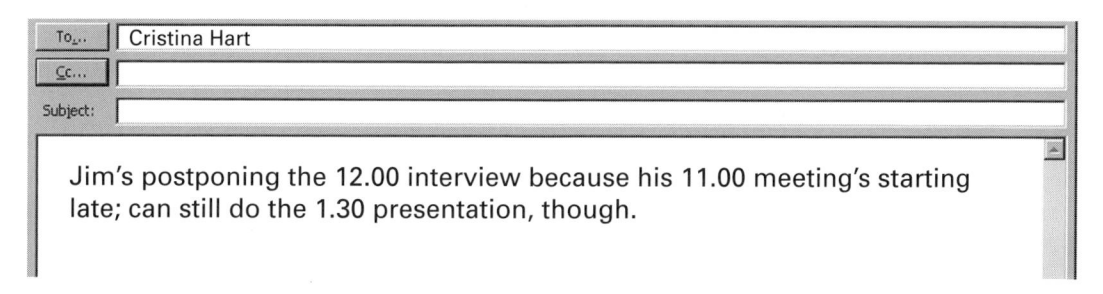

To: Cristina Hart
Cc:
Subject:

Jim's postponing the 12.00 interview because his 11.00 meeting's starting late; can still do the 1.30 presentation, though.

Which arrangement is taking place at the time that was planned?

- **A** the meeting
- **B** the interview
- **C** the presentation

5

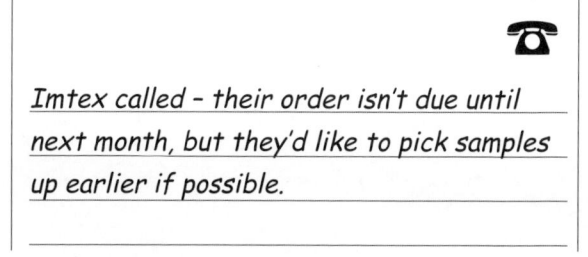

Imtex called – their order isn't due until next month, but they'd like to pick samples up earlier if possible.

Imtex wants to

- **A** postpone an arrangement.
- **B** collect some items.
- **C** change an order.

PART TWO

Questions 6–10

- Look at the notice below. It shows the companies with offices in the Royal Commercial building.
- For questions **6–10**, decide which company (**A–H**) each person on the opposite page needs.
- For each question, mark one letter (**A–H**) on your Answer Sheet.
- Do not use any letter more than once.

The Royal Commercial Building
Liverpool

A	Masters & Cotgrove – Accountants & Investment Consultants	1st Floor
B	Pershore Plc – Travel, Hotel and Car Hire Agency	2nd Floor
C	Medics Unlimited – Health Insurance	3rd Floor
D	Marine Express Shipping Company	4th Floor
E	PBS – Electrical Engineers	5th Floor
F	Parnell & Lewis – International Legal Advisors	6th Floor
G	Alex Conrad & Sons – Commercial Property Agents	7th Floor
H	Fabfoods – Catering Personnel & Kitchen Supplies	8th Floor

6 Dr Shah wants to arrange for medical supplies and electronic equipment to be sent out to his clinic in Bangladesh.

7 Crockfords, an international law firm, needs lighting and cooking equipment installed in the canteen at its new offices.

8 Lia Kandinsky needs new premises for her internet company that finds hotels and flights for customers.

9 Dr Munroe needs to get to Sydney, Australia, for a World Health Organisation conference on food and health.

10 Crombie's Fastfoods wants help with checking all its financial transactions for the last three years.

Test 4

PART THREE

Questions 11–15

- Look at the charts below. They show the number of days lost because of staff absence in eight companies, from June to September in both 2002 and 2003.
- Which chart does each sentence (**11–15**) on the opposite page describe?
- For each sentence, mark one letter (**A–H**) on your Answer Sheet.
- Do not use any letter more than once.

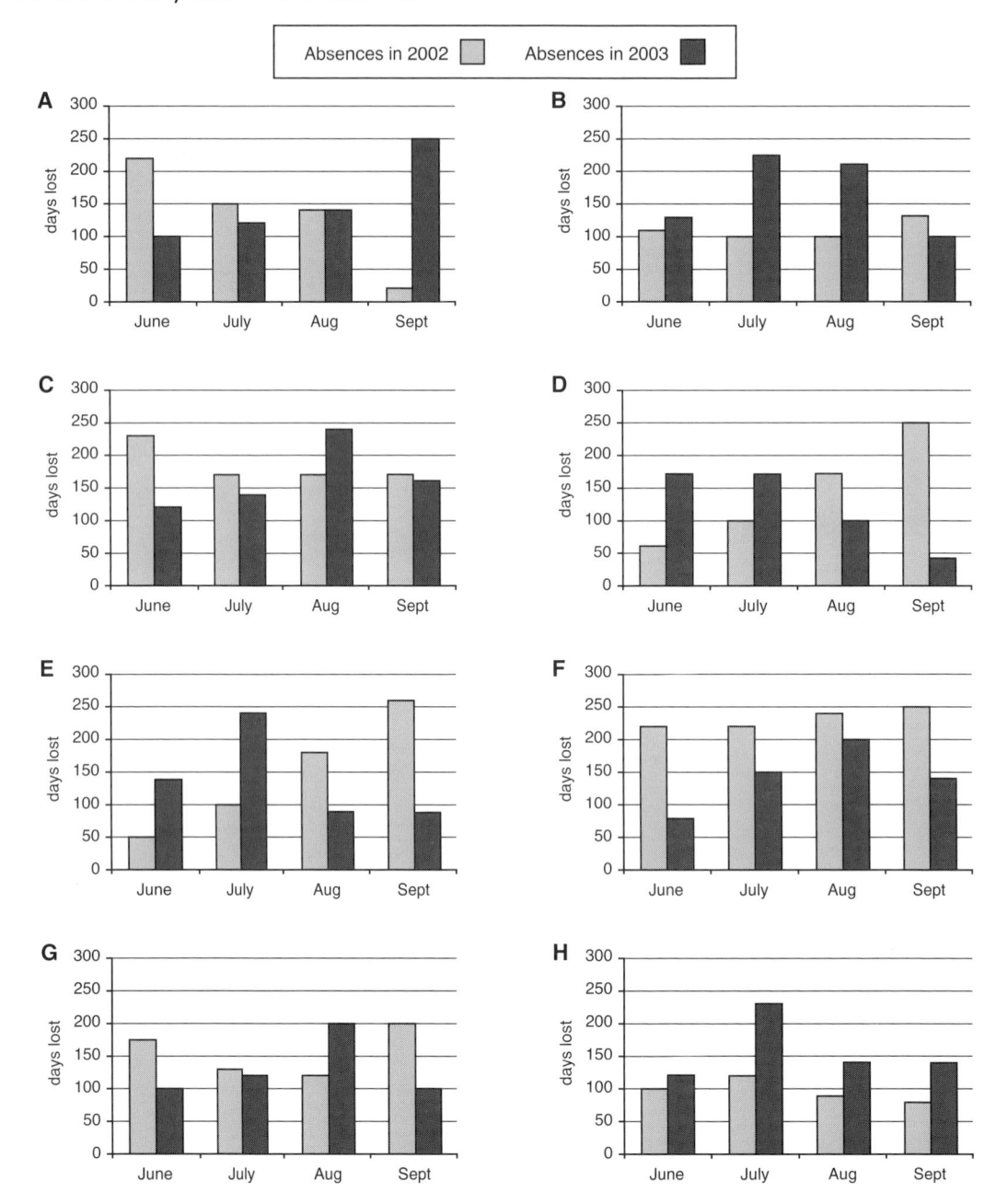

Absences in 2002   Absences in 2003

11 The number of absences rose between June and August 2003, when it equalled the previous September's high, before dropping to half that level.

12 In 2003, absences peaked in August, though still not reaching the level of the previous year, when absences showed little change throughout the period.

13 Absences in 2002 varied little, but in 2003 they rose sharply in July, dropping considerably the next month and staying unchanged in September.

14 2003 absences first overtook 2002's figures in August, but they ended the period slightly below the level of the same month in the previous year.

15 2002 saw a continuing increase in absences, unlike 2003, when two months had the same low level after a sharp rise in July.

PART FOUR

Questions 16–22

- Read the review below of a book about interviewing job applicants.
- Are sentences **16–22** on the opposite page 'Right' or 'Wrong'? If there is not enough information to answer 'Right' or 'Wrong', choose 'Doesn't say'.
- For each sentence (**16–22**), mark one letter (**A**, **B** or **C**) on your Answer Sheet.

Interviewing Skills, by Hazel Conway

The aim of interviewing is to fill vacancies with suitable people, and Hazel Conway points out that if all interviewers were skilled, far fewer people would be given jobs they cannot do, and then leave soon afterwards. It is generally recognised that the cost of recruiting a replacement can equal an annual salary, but it is a weakness of Conway's book that it does not deal with the costs that ineffective interviewing techniques can lead to.

Conway claims that the traditional 'question and answer' interview between two people depends too much on whether the interviewer likes the candidate, and not enough on whether he or she has the skills necessary for the job.

Interviewing Skills usefully covers everything an employer needs to know about preparing for and holding interviews, such as researching the applicant's work experience. Surprisingly, Conway differs from many writers in considering that applicants' personal interests should play no part in decisions concerning appointments. Many might also disagree with the book's ideas on how to reject unsuccessful candidates.

While *Interviewing Skills* would be helpful for someone about to interview job applicants for the first time, it has little to offer anyone experienced in the activity.

16 Hazel Conway claims that an improvement in interviewing would reduce staff turnover.

   A Right   **B** Wrong   **C** Doesn't say

17 Hazel Conway gives details of the costs resulting from poor interviewing.

   A Right   **B** Wrong   **C** Doesn't say

18 According to Hazel Conway, at least two people should represent the company in an interview.

   A Right   **B** Wrong   **C** Doesn't say

19 Hazel Conway argues that interviewers should pay more attention to their feelings about the applicant.

   A Right   **B** Wrong   **C** Doesn't say

20 Hazel Conway stresses the importance of finding out about candidates' interests.

   A Right   **B** Wrong   **C** Doesn't say

21 The book contains advice on turning down applicants.

   A Right   **B** Wrong   **C** Doesn't say

22 The book contains some useful advice for job applicants preparing for interviews.

   A Right   **B** Wrong   **C** Doesn't say

PART FIVE

Questions 23–28

- Read the article below about a furniture retailer.
- For each question (**23–28**), on the opposite page, choose the correct answer.
- Mark one letter (**A**, **B** or **C**) on your Answer Sheet.

A Bright Future

The furniture retailer, CHR, which has produced disappointing results recently, said that market conditions were at last improving. Sales rose by 6.7% in the final quarter of 2003, after falling by 5.3% in the three months between July and September, and by 7.4% in the previous quarter.

Tony Graham, the managing director, said that, although the market remained competitive, orders had reached their highest level ever and with this promising news he thought that profit margins would reach 10% before the end of the next financial year. The company is also benefiting from the current low interest rates charged by the banks. Further savings were made when the company increased the proportion of furniture that it produced itself. This followed its takeover in April of the Tristar Furniture factory, which was suffering from serious financial problems.

CHR will continue its expansion programme this year and expects to add four new stores to the existing fifty. These will all be in the north-east of England, where it currently has only one store. The company aims eventually to have eighty large stores nationwide and then to concentrate on opening a number of smaller ones.

This positive news was delivered together with the announcement of a 12% drop in profits to £26 million on sales of £295 million for the financial year. This fall was not as bad as forecasted – several analysts thought profits would be less than £10 million.

Before becoming managing director of CHR, Graham had worked for Darnton Paints. Though Darnton Paints was once a leader in its field, it was in serious financial difficulties when Graham joined the company. Within three years, however, he had turned the company's annual losses into a £10 million profit. He is beginning to do the same at CHR.

23 Between April and June 2003, CHR's sales

   A   fell by 5.3%.
   B   rose by 6.7%.
   C   fell by 7.4%.

24 Why does the managing director feel positive about the company?

   A   It has beaten the competition.
   B   It has lowered interest rates on purchases.
   C   It has received a record number of orders.

25 The takeover of Tristar helped CHR

   A   to solve all its financial problems.
   B   to make more of its own furniture.
   C   to sell a wider range of goods.

26 CHR plans to open

   A   more stores in the north-east of England.
   B   eighty large stores over the next few years.
   C   a number of small stores next year.

27 Profits this year were

   A   worse than expected.
   B   the same as expected.
   C   better than expected.

28 What do CHR and Darnton Paints have in common?

   A   They have both seen an improvement in their financial position.
   B   They both used to be leading companies in their fields.
   C   They were both performing badly due to increased competition.

PART SIX

Questions 29–40

- Read the email below about advertising.
- Choose the correct word to fill each gap from **A**, **B** or **C** on the opposite page.
- For each question (**29–40**), mark one letter (**A**, **B** or **C**) on your Answer Sheet.

From: Gillian Otwell
To: Marketing Manager
Sent: 20 November 2004
Subject: New Magazine

You said recently you'd like to increase our advertising: here's a suggestion. (**29**) .... a sales meeting I attended yesterday, I heard that a new weekly magazine for business people (**30**) .... launched last month by a well-known publishing group. It targets (**31**) .... who run small businesses but don't buy business magazines. It's free, and (**32**) .... should mean it'll be popular. It's got sixteen pages at the (**33**) ...., and the plan is to increase it (**34**) .... sixty-four.

There are (**35**) .... many business magazines on the market that maybe there isn't (**36**) .... for another one. But, (**37**) .... I said, this one's free, and most of the others are quite expensive.

(**38**) .... else you'll be particularly (**39**) .... about is that the advertising rates are the lowest I've seen. (**40**) .... we have a smaller budget this year, we should easily be able to afford them.

Hope this will be useful to you.

29	**A** By	**B** During	**C** Within
30	**A** had	**B** did	**C** was
31	**A** them	**B** these	**C** those
32	**A** that	**B** what	**C** which
33	**A** time	**B** moment	**C** point
34	**A** to	**B** at	**C** on
35	**A** very	**B** too	**C** so
36	**A** gap	**B** area	**C** room
37	**A** as	**B** how	**C** when
38	**A** Everything	**B** Something	**C** Anything
39	**A** interested	**B** pleased	**C** attracted
40	**A** Though	**B** Because	**C** However

PART SEVEN

Questions 41–45

- Read the memo and the advertisement below.
- Complete the form on the opposite page.
- Write a word or phrase (in CAPITAL LETTERS) or a number on lines **41–45** on your Answer Sheet.

Colston Newland

MEMO

To: Pam Gray
From: Jim Moore
Date: 20.11.04
Subject: Training course

I need some new ideas for when I'm trying to sell to potential customers, so I've decided to attend the course that Business Solutions runs on presentations. The complete course would be perfect, but I really can't spare the time – I'm sure the other one will be fine.

Finance are willing to pay by cheque if necessary, but would be happier if the company accepted a bank transfer.

Could you organise it, please? The person to contact is Kamila Mudrazija.

BUSINESS SOLUTIONS
For all your training needs

We are currently offering the following programmes:

- Selling by Telephone
- The Secrets of Customer Care
- New Ideas for Negotiating
- Perfect Presentations

Complete courses – two days; Fast-track option – half a day; reductions for group bookings.

Application for Training

Complete the form below to book a place on one of our courses.

Full name of participant: **(41)** ....

Company: **(42)** ....

Title of course: **(43)** ....

Length of course: **(44)** ....

Preferred method of payment: **(45)** ....

Test 4

WRITING

PART ONE

Question 46

- In the office where you work, there is a problem with the computers.
- Write an **email** to Bob Hargreaves, the IT engineer at your company:
  - saying which office you work in
  - describing what is wrong with the computers
  - requesting repairs as soon as possible.
- Write **30–40** words on your Answer Sheet.

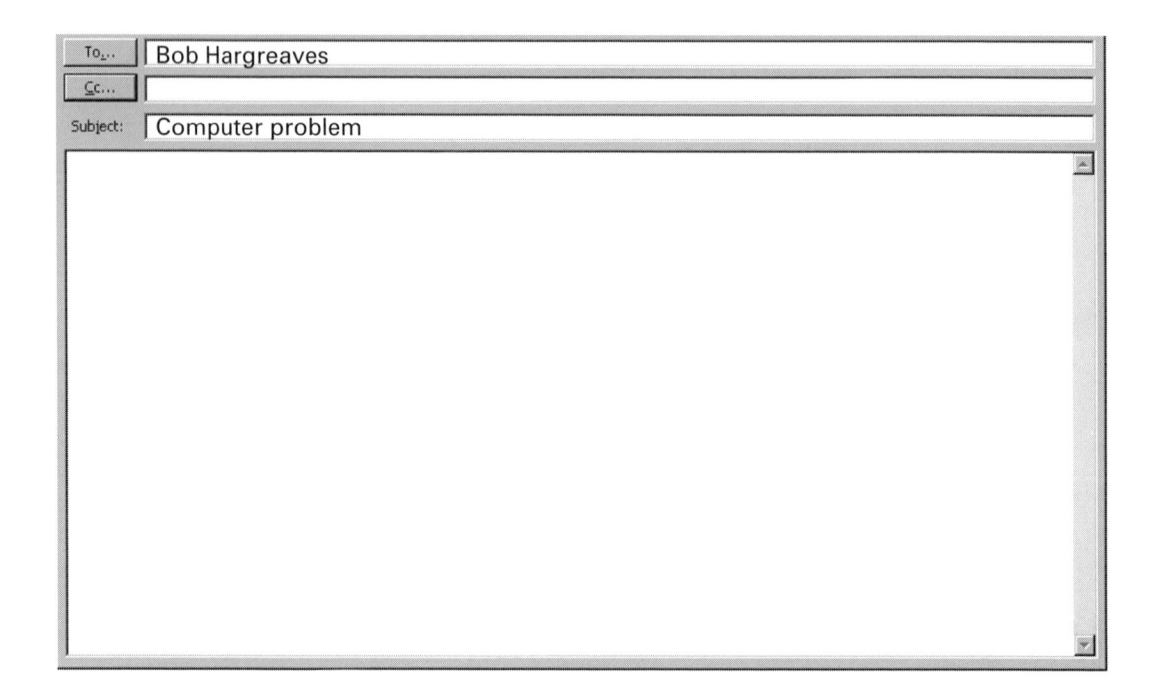

To... Bob Hargreaves
Cc...
Subject: Computer problem

Writing

PART TWO

Question 47

- Read the memo below from the CEO of your company.

MEMO

To: International Sales staff
From: CEO
Date: 30/10/04
Subject: 50th anniversary celebration

I think it would be a good idea to include some of our overseas clients on the guest list for the formal event we are planning as part of the company's 50th anniversary celebrations.

Could all International Sales staff write to their most important clients to invite them to the event.

- Write a **letter** to an overseas client, Mrs Johannson:
  - inviting her to the event
  - giving her the date of the event
  - giving details of what will happen at the event
  - explaining what overnight accommodation is available.
- Write **60–80** words on your Answer Sheet.
- Do not include any postal addresses.

Dear Mrs Johannson,

Test 4

LISTENING Approximately 40 minutes (including 10 minutes' transfer time)

LISTENING

PART ONE

Questions 1–8

- For questions **1–8** you will hear eight short recordings.
- For each question, mark **one** letter (**A**, **B** or **C**) for the correct answer.

> **Example:**
>
> Who is Emily going to write to?
>
> **A** the staff
> **B** the supplier
> **C** the clients
>
> The answer is **A**.

- After you have listened once, replay each recording.

1 When will the meeting take place?

JUNE					
	1	2	3	4	5	6
7	8	9	10	11	⑫	13
14	15	16	17	18	19	20
21	22	23	24	25	26	27
28	29	30				

A

JUNE					
	1	2	3	4	5	6
7	8	9	10	11	12	13
14	⑮	16	17	18	19	20
21	22	23	24	25	26	27
28	29	30				

B

JUNE					
	1	2	3	4	5	6
7	8	9	10	11	12	13
14	15	16	17	18	19	20
21	22	㉓	24	25	26	27
28	29	30				

C

Listening

2 Which part of the woman's computer is causing a problem?

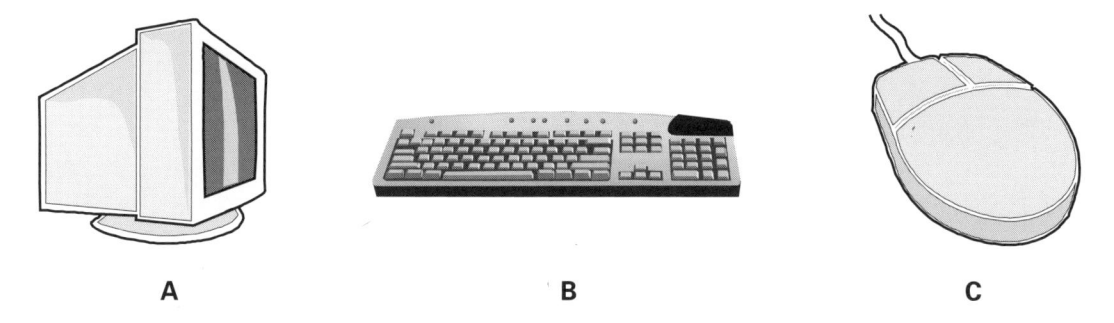

A			B			C

3 Which chart shows last year's sales figures?

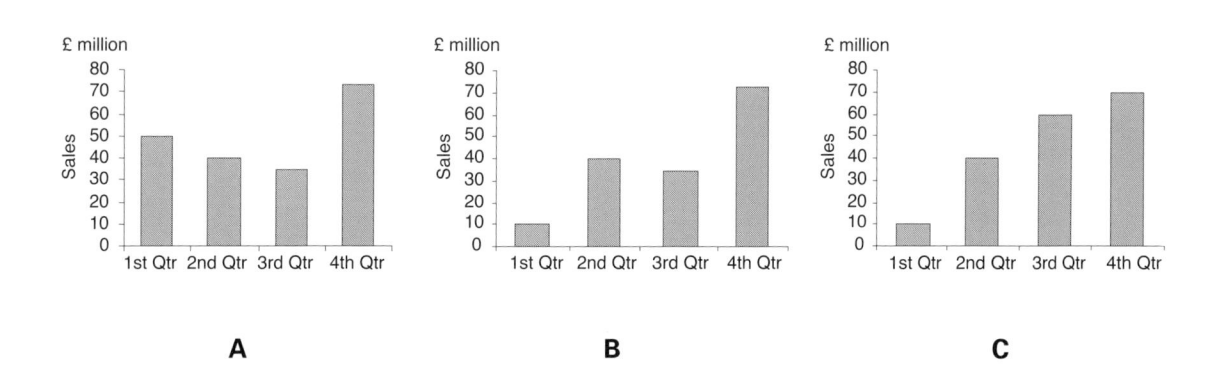

A			B			C

4 What is the lowest price the man can buy the machine for?

$10,000			$13,000			$14,500

A			B			C

111

Test 4

5 What will help the company to increase production?

    A offering overtime work

    B reducing packaging

    C hiring temporary staff

6 Which chart shows the company's spending on training last year?

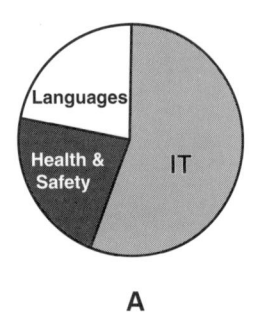

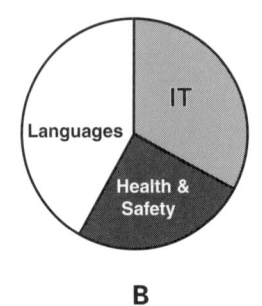

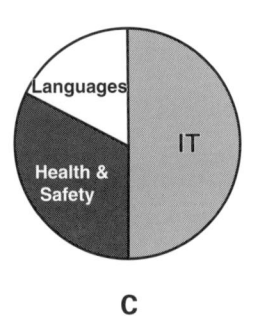

    A   B   C

7 Where should staff leave office cars?

    A in front of the office

    B at the back of the building

    C outside Reception

8 Who does the man think will get the job?

    A Rachel

    B Anna

    C Laura

Listening

PART TWO

Questions 9–15

- Look at the notes below.
- Some information is missing.
- You will hear Ann Simpson of Blackwell Sports talking to a journalist.
- For each question (**9–15**), fill in the missing information in the numbered space using a **word**, **numbers** or **letters**.
- After you have listened once, replay the recording.

NOTES FOR ARTICLE ON BLACKWELL SPORTS

Increase in turnover for current year:	**(9)** £ .... million
Merged with:	**(10)** .... Outdoor Equipment
Best-selling tent:	**(11)** ....
Number of stores in Britain now:	**(12)** ....
Number of stores opening early next year:	**(13)** ....
Sales of women's sports clothing: increase of:	**(14)** .... % in last year and a half
Ann Simpson's mobile number:	**(15)** 07790 ....

113

Test 4

PART THREE

Questions 16–22

- Look at the notes about an American businessman called Matthew Webb, who is working in the UK for a company called Electra.
- Some information is missing.
- You will hear part of a presentation describing his working life.
- For each question (**16–22**), fill in the missing information in the numbered space using **one** or **two** words.
- After you have listened once, replay the recording.

MATTHEW WEBB

Electra company sells (16) ....

At college, Matthew started (17) .... course

Star Stores

Position in company: (18) ....

Increased market share due to improvements in: (19) ....

Electra

Joined Electra in order to develop his (20) ....

Present position at Electra UK: (21) ....

Electra has higher UK turnover because of more (22) ....

PART FOUR

Questions 23–30

- You will hear a radio interview with Beth Hatfield, the Director of Jumpstart, a recruitment agency.
- For each question (**23–30**), mark **one** letter (**A**, **B** or **C**) for the correct answer.
- After you have listened once, replay the recording.

23 Beth Hatfield lost her job because the company she worked for

    A had financial difficulties.
    B lost a major contract.
    C was taken over.

24 When Beth lost her job, she was very worried about

    A close colleagues.
    B her own future.
    C a major client.

25 Dryden Limited helped Beth to set up Jumpstart by providing

    A office space.
    B office equipment.
    C office staff.

26 A friend called Thomas Beck advised Beth to

    A concentrate on one business idea only.
    B invest heavily in marketing her new business.
    C make full use of her existing business contacts.

27 Beth financed Jumpstart by

    A borrowing money from the bank.
    B finding a business partner.
    C selling her own house.

Test 4

28 Jumpstart found its first recruits by advertising

    A   in newspapers.
    B   in magazines.
    C   on the internet.

29 All the people that Jumpstart finds work for must

    A   be highly qualified in marketing.
    B   have relevant professional experience.
    C   be free to travel.

30 Which aspect of setting up Jumpstart was most difficult for Beth?

    A   finding companies who required temporary staff
    B   recruiting the right quality of marketing personnel
    C   persuading companies to agree to her charges

You now have 10 minutes to transfer your answers to your Answer Sheet.

SPEAKING 12 minutes

SAMPLE SPEAKING TASKS

PART ONE

In this part, the interlocutor asks questions to each of the candidates in turn. You have to give information about yourself and express personal opinions.

PART TWO

In this part of the test, you are asked to give a short talk on a business topic. You have to choose one of the topics from the two below and then talk for about one minute. You have one minute to prepare your ideas.

A: What is important when . . . ?

Buying products on the internet

- Safe payment system
- Wide choice of products
- Quick delivery

B: What is important when . . . ?

Organising job interviews

- Time available
- Number of interviewers
- Preparing questions

Test 4

PART THREE

In this part of the test, the examiner reads out a scenario and gives you some prompt material in the form of pictures or words. You have 30 seconds to look at the task prompt, an example of which is below, and then about two minutes to discuss the scenario with your partner. After that, the examiner will ask you more questions related to the topic.

For **two** or **three** candidates

Scenario

> I'm going to describe a situation.
>
> **The company you work for wants to launch an advertising campaign to increase the sales of a brand of sports shoes. Talk together for about two minutes* about some of the ways to advertise the product and decide which two would be best.**
>
> Here are some ideas to help you.

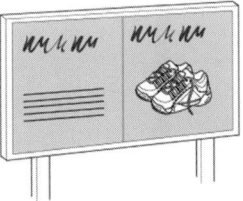

*three minutes for groups of three candidates.

Prompt material

Follow-on questions

- In what other ways could the company promote the brand? (Why?)
- What influences you most when you buy sports shoes? (Why?)
- Do you think advertising always increases sales? (Why?)
- What makes an advertisement effective? (Why?/Why not?)
- Apart from promotion, in what other ways might a company increase sales? (Why?)

KEY

Test 1   Reading

Part 1

1 C   2 B   3 A   4 C   5 C

Part 2

6 D   7 H   8 C   9 B   10 E

Part 3

11 B   12 G   13 H   14 F   15 D

Part 4

16 B   17 A   18 A   19 B   20 A
21 C   22 B

Part 5

23 B   24 C   25 B   26 A   27 A
28 C

Part 6

29 A   30 B   31 C   32 C   33 A
34 B   35 A   36 A   37 C   38 A
39 C   40 B

Part 7

41 DESIGN ASSISTANT (IN SPORTSWEAR)
42 24(TH) NOVEMBER(2003) / 24/11(/03).
43 SPORTSWEAR
44 COMPUTER SKILLS(S)
45 (THE) LOCAL (NEWS)PAPER

Test 1 Writing

Part 1

Sample A

> Hello James
>
> I must cancle our meeting on 25 November. The reason for the cancellation is, I will attend the meeting with John Brown, the Sales Manager.
>
> He can meet us on 28 November, is it ok for you?
>
> Joana

Band 3
The first content point is not addressed. Otherwise, the message is clear. However, the tone of the email is not always appropriate.

Sample B

> Dear Mr. Lewis,
>
> I'm afraid, I must cancel our meeting. I must go to London. We have problems there. So I would say we make another date for our meeting. What do you think about the 10 December 2003? Please give me an answer soon.
>
> Kind regards
>
> Katja Stein

Band 5
All the content points are covered clearly. The candidate demonstrates good language control and uses a wide range of appropriate phrases to achieve a friendly, respectful tone.

Part 2

Sample C

> Dear Mr Trellis
>
> Thank you for your letter of 22 November about our Business Award.
>
> I am writing to inform you about topic; result 2003 and goals 2004. I would like conference room and OHP. There will be 40 participants, also your staff can be there. I would be greateful if you could prepare topic "goals 2004"
>
> I look forward to hearing from you soon.
>
> Yours sincerely
>
> Felipe Ruiz

Band 2
The letter is appropriately laid out, making good use of functional language, but with poor linkage between sentences. Content points one and four are not achieved.

Sample D

> Dear Mr Trellis,
>
> I am writting you to thank you for the Business 2003 Award. We will be present on February 19.
>
> We will speak about our new plant.
>
> We will need a map of the world, a big television with video and a space to put our marketing products.
>
> Could I take with me some members of my staff?
>
> It would be very grateful from you.
>
> Yours sincerely
>
> Sue

Band 4
All the content points are achieved and the format and style of the letter are appropriate. The range of vocabulary used is more than adequate and good use is made of functional language. Some errors do occur, but these are non-impeding.

Test 1 Listening

Part 1

1 C 2 A 3 C 4 A 5 B 6 B
7 B 8 C

Part 2

9 ALFORDS
10 GE24601
11 37 (MACHINES)
12 (£)1978
13 (£)45
14 8 (HOURS)
15 (OUR) (USUAL) 29 (DAYS)

Part 3

16 RIVERSIDE (CLOTHING LTD)
17 (THE) CHIEF EXECUTIVE/CE/CEO
18 (NEAR) (THE) AIRPORT
19 (THE) MANUFACTURING (SPACE/AREA)
20 (NEW) (STAFF) CAR PARK/PARKING/ STAFF PARKING
21 CHILDREN'S (CLOTHES)/CHILDREN'S WEAR/CHILDREN
22 AUSTRALIA

Part 4

23 C 24 C 25 A 26 A 27 A
28 B 29 C 30 C

Tapescript

Listening Test 1

This is the Business English Certificate Preliminary 3, Listening Test 1.

Part One. Questions 1 to 8.

For questions 1–8, you will hear eight short recordings. For each question, mark one letter (A, B or C) for the correct answer.

Here is an example: Who is Emily going to write to?

[pause]

Man: Emily, that supplier we use has become very unreliable, and we've decided to look for another one.
Woman: Seems a good idea.
Man: We don't need to inform our clients, but could you send a note round to all our departments when we've decided who to replace the supplier with?
Woman: Yes, of course.

[pause]

The answer is A.

Now we are ready to start.

After you have listened once, replay each recording.

[pause]

One: *When will the meeting be?*

[pause]

Man: Sarah, can you fix a date for us to discuss the new advertising campaign with Nick Bradshaw? It'll have to be next week. I can manage the twelfth, fourteenth or fifteenth, as long as it's after three-thirty.
Woman: Right, but Nick said he'd be away until the fourteenth, so it'll have to be the following day.
Man: That'll be fine.

[pause]

Two: *Which office suppliers are they going to use?*

[pause]

Key

Woman: This latest order from Office Network is very expensive. Have you thought about changing suppliers?
Man: Well, I did think about it. But Excel Products wouldn't give us any discount and A-Grade Service want cash on delivery, so let's just leave things as they are.

[pause]

Three: Which line shows productivity correctly?

[pause]

Man: These figures are interesting, aren't they? I expected to see the highest productivity in the earliest part of the day, and the lowest at the end.
Woman: But . . . in fact, the peak time's just before midday, isn't it?
Man: And performance is better at the end of the day than it is after lunch. I imagined it'd be the other way round.

[pause]

Four: What is the correct length?

[pause]

Man: Hello, I'm calling from Brent Hardware. There's an error in our catalogue, and we missed it when we were proofreading. It's on page twenty-six.
Woman: Oh?
Man: It says the length is five forty but it should be four twenty millimetres.
Woman: Right. Oh yes, I see. The height is still four hundred and fifty-two, isn't it?
Man: That's right.
Woman: OK, we'll re-do that page.

[pause]

Five: What does the woman want to do about the meeting?

[pause]

Woman: Ben . . . hello, Emily Jones here. I'm calling about the project meeting . . .
Man: . . . on the fifteenth of May?
Woman: Yes . . . I think that date's going to be too soon – I still haven't got the figures I need from the contractor.
Man: Do you want to put it off then?
Woman: Please. I'll get back to you about alternative dates.

[pause]

Six: What time will Mr Johnstone arrive?

[pause]

Man: It's Peter here from Executive Cars. I'm collecting a Mr Johnstone from the States. His flight arrived at fourteen forty-five, but he still hasn't come through customs.
Woman: Sorry . . . yes. We've had a message to say he took a different flight. He gets in at sixteen fifty. Can you wait?
Man: OK. The next flight I'm meeting isn't until twenty-one ten. I'll get something to eat . . .

[pause]

Seven: Which chart shows where the company's goods are made?

[pause]

. . . and the majority of our parts are made outside the US with sixty per cent manufactured in Asia, a smaller amount, just ten per cent, made in Eastern Europe and a further five per cent in Scandinavia; the remaining quarter are produced here in the US . . .

[pause]

Eight: Which task is urgent?

[pause]

Man: Sarah, are you busy?
Woman: Not very. Have you signed the letters I put on your desk?
Man: They're in the post. The thing is, there's a problem at the Barcelona office. We've got several faxes from them that need answering at once. Could you do that?
Woman: No problem. After that, shall we check our diaries for this week?
Man: Good idea.

[pause]

That is the end of Part One.

[pause]

Part Two. Questions 9 to 15.

Look at the notes below.

Some information is missing.

You will hear an engineering manager giving a secretary some information about a quotation.

For each question 9–15, fill in the missing information in the numbered space using a word, numbers or letters.

Test 1

After you have listened once, replay the recording.

You have ten seconds to read through the notes.

[pause]

Now listen, and fill in the missing information.

Woman: Jim Morgan's office.
Man: Sally, Jim here.
Woman: Hello. How was the visit to that company interested in a service contract?
Man: Good. Could you do a quote to send them today?
Woman: Sure.
Man: It's to go to Alfords International.
Woman: Is that double L?
Man: . . . one. A-L-F-O-R-D-S. Their address is on my desk.
Woman: Right, thanks. Have you got a reference number?
Man: G-E-two-four-six-O-one.
Woman: What equipment do they have for servicing? Does it include their office machines?
Man: Well, they've got nearly five hundred, so another company is looking after those. They want us to service the thirty-seven machines in the packing department.
Woman: OK.
Man: Now, I've worked out an annual charge . . . cheaper than their current supplier. We're quoting one thousand nine hundred and seventy-eight pounds, that's including tax. Then there's charges for emergency work.
Woman: Is that the usual forty-five pounds call-out charge?
Man: Mmm . . . I didn't reduce the price on that – it's standard.
Woman: Fine.
Man: Also, I gave them a guaranteed response time – at the moment they have to wait up to twenty-four hours for an engineer to visit. I promised they wouldn't have to wait more than eight hours if they chose us.
Woman: OK. Is that everything?
Man: Almost. Payment terms – I didn't negotiate on these. Their current supplier only gives twenty days, so our usual twenty-nine is already much better.
Woman: Right, I'll get . . .

[pause]

Now listen to the recording again.

[pause]

That is the end of Part Two. You now have ten seconds to check your answers.

[pause]

Part Three. Questions 16 to 22.

Look at the notes about the launch of a new clothing company.

Some information is missing.

You will hear part of a welcoming talk by the company's Managing Director.

For each question 16–22, fill in the missing information in the numbered space using one or two words.

After you have listened once, replay the recording.

You have ten seconds to read through the notes.

[pause]

Now listen, and fill in the missing information.

[pause]

Man: Good morning, everyone, and welcome to the launch of our new company. This is a special day for us, now we have merged with Sinclairs to become Riverside Clothing Limited, and we are confident that our success at selling our own brand of clothing will continue.
  There have been some important staff changes. Our previous Chief Executive, Simon Marsh, has moved on to become MD of another company, so congratulations to our Sales Manager, David Shaw, who will become Chief Executive. We wish him every success in his new role.
  The position of the new premises here was carefully chosen so that we would be near the airport, instead of being in a city centre, like a lot of other factories.
  These premises are far bigger. Although our sales area has remained about the same and we have slightly more room for design workshops, it is the manufacturing area that we have expanded the most.
  As you can see, this is a very exciting time for us and we will continue to improve our facilities for staff. There will now be plenty of space to build a new staff car park, as parking has always been a problem. That'll be completed in the spring. However, the staff canteen is now open and I hope you will be joining us for lunch there later.
  Now that we've moved, we intend to expand into two new areas of the clothing industry.

Key

In addition to our existing adults' range, we are ready to start on a range of children's clothes. These will be in production by next month, followed later in the year by a new range of sportswear.

We already have a strong market for the range – in America and Japan, but will be targeting Australia next, which is an unknown export market for us.

Now . . .

[pause]

Now listen to the recording again.

[pause]

That is the end of Part Three. You now have twenty seconds to check your answers.

[pause]

Part Four. Questions 23 to 30.

You will hear a radio interview with George Johnson, Managing Director of Media-X, an organisation which invests in internet companies.

For each question 23–30, mark one letter (A, B or C) for the correct answer.

After you have listened once, replay the recording.

You have forty-five seconds to read through the questions.

[pause]

Now listen, and mark A, B or C.

Woman: Good afternoon, and welcome to *Working Day*. Today we're going to meet George Johnson, Managing Director of Media-X, an investment company always in the news these days. Hello, George, welcome to the programme.
Man: Hello, Sarah.
Woman: First of all, a question I'm sure you're often asked. Why is the company called Media-X? Has it got anything to do with film or television?
Man: Not really. But we wanted to get away from the serious image of money and banking, and wanted something that people wouldn't forget. We also considered names connected with e-commerce and the internet, but in the end we decided we wanted something more general. And Media-X seemed a good choice.
Woman: Interesting. Now let's get on to what Media-X actually does. You were one of the first in the business to provide financial as well as technical advice, weren't you, for new internet and software companies?
Man: Well, I wasn't as far-sighted as a lot of people, especially in America. When I first heard about the internet in nineteen ninety-one, I thought it would be only used for education. But I actually decided to set up Media-X the following year, when I realised that new software was already making it easier to use. So I suppose that was quite early on – compared to most other Europeans, that is.
Woman: But what about before that? Tell us something about your early career.
Man: I studied economics at university and then joined a large international bank as a trainee manager, eventually becoming a vice-president. Towards the end of that period, I also became a director of a small software company my brother was setting up.
Woman: So business runs in the family, then?
Man: That's right. My father has a well-established office supplies company, so, apart from the financial side, he also knows a lot about warehouses, storage and delivery systems, which are very important in the e-commerce business. I rely on his opinion a lot when I'm trying to decide whether or not to invest in new ventures.
Woman: So, tell us about the companies you help. I'm sure you get lots of requests for funding sent to you.
Man: Yes, we receive about three hundred proposals a year. We examine them all, discuss them, then decide which to go with. About two hundred are worth considering in detail, with maybe a hundred being finally selected.
Woman: What would you say makes a successful proposal?
Man: Well, we look for a number of things. But, before anything else, we have to be sure there's a clear demand for what the company intends to provide. Of course, then we have to consider other things like a strong business plan behind the proposal and, of course, the people at the top – they've got to be worth investing in.
Woman: You mentioned before that you don't only provide the money for starting new businesses. What other services do you provide?
Man: We're not in a position to provide software programmes, technical details, things like that, or information about possible markets. Where we can help is by making sure that companies

know what to charge for their goods and services so that everything is on a healthy basis.
Woman: And you've certainly enjoyed some recent successes, haven't you?
Man: Well, yes, some of the British companies we've supported have been doing rather well – TravelDeals-dot-com is now one of the leading travel companies here in Britain.
Woman: And OrderFree-dot-com is also doing well. It's gone into the American market, hasn't it?
Man: That's right. It's very promising.
Woman: And then there's NetTrade-dot-com, another of the UK companies you funded. Do you think they'll follow OrderFree's example and set up abroad?
Man: I doubt that very much. Only time will tell, of course . . .
Woman: That seems a good point on which to end. Thank you very much, George Johnson, for a very interesting . . .

[pause]

Now listen to the recording again.

[pause]

That is the end of Part Four. You now have ten minutes to transfer your answers to your Answer Sheet.

[pause]

Note: Teacher, stop the recording here and time ten minutes. Remind students when there is **one** minute remaining.

That is the end of the test.

Test 2 Reading

Part 1
1 A   2 B   3 A   4 C   5 C

Part 2
6 H   7 G   8 A   9 F   10 C

Part 3
11 C   12 H   13 B   14 G   15 F

Part 4
16 B   17 C   18 A   19 B   20 B
21 C   22 A

Part 5
23 C   24 B   25 B   26 C   27 A
28 C

Part 6
29 C   30 A   31 A   32 B   33 A
34 A   35 B   36 A   37 C   38 C
39 B   40 C

Part 7
41 (MRS, MS, ETC.) SANDRA COOKE
42 QUALITY CONTROL (DEPT/DEPARTMENT)
43 DESK (SIZE)
44 RIGHTWAY SUPPLIES (PO BOX 2059)
45 10(TH) APRIL (2004)/10/04(/04)

Test 2 Writing

Part 1

Sample A

> Could you allow me to go to the conference, please. I am very interesting in sales and it should be an advantage for my career. If you agree, I could go by car with my colleague to reduce the cost. Thanks

Band 4
Although this response achieves the three content points, the reader would be unsure which conference is being referred to.

Sample B

> Dear Mr Carpenter,
>
> I would like required you attention on the sale conference in New York next month. In fact I think I could meeting own customers and make discover the new technologies of the laboratory.
>
> I know you a reduce of cost policy, but if I take a old charter and I stay one day-in order to two days and that I launch a sandwich.

Band 2
All the content points are attempted, and achieved to some extent, but overall the message is inadequate.

Key

Part 2

Sample C

> Dear Mr French,
>
> I am writing to thank you for your letter and for the interesting opportunity of publicity you are offering to our company.
>
> Therefore, I will be pleased to meet you for an interview. Would Thursday 10th April at 10am be convenient for you?
>
> The company operates in the fashion market and our main activity is producing high quality women trousers.
>
> I would be very grateful if you could inform me when the directory will be published.
>
> I look forward to hearing from you in the near future.
>
> Yours sincerely,

Band 5

All the content points are achieved in this response, which is written in an appropriate register and format, and displays confident control and a good range of language.

Sample D

> Dear Mr French,
>
> I am writing you this letter to make an appointment for an interview with you. In this interview I am going to present my company and I am going to give you details for the organisation of your company.
>
> Our company have many ideas to redruce line of work in other company for redrucing money.
>
> Please find enclosed the agenda of my company and feel free if you have any questions.
>
> I am looking forward to hearing from you with appointment for the interview.
>
> Your truly

Band 1

The task has been misunderstood and much of this response is therefore irrelevant. Only the first content point has been achieved.

Test 2 Listening

Part 1

1 A 2 C 3 A 4 B 5 B 6 B
7 C 8 B

Part 2

9 25(TH)
10 INTERNATIONAL
11 535
12 DAUGHTON
13 10.30 (AM)
14 (£)325
15 0144377

Part 3

16 RESEARCH MANAGER
17 BUILDING EQUIPMENT
18 STANDARD CONSTRUCTION
19 CHEMISTRY
20 MARKETING ASSISTANT
21 FRENCH (AND) SPANISH
22 DECEMBER/DEC

Part 4

23 B 24 A 25 C 26 B 27 C
28 B 29 A 30 B

Tapescript

Listening Test 2

This is the Business English Certificate Preliminary 3, Listening Test 2.

Part One. Questions 1 to 8.

For questions 1–8, you will hear eight short recordings. For each question, mark one letter (A, B or C) for the correct answer.

Here is an example: Who is Emily going to write to?

[pause]

Man: Emily, that supplier we use has become very unreliable, and we've decided to look for another one.
Woman: Seems a good idea.
Man: We don't need to inform our clients, but could you send a note round to all our departments when we've decided who to replace the supplier with?

Woman: Yes, of course.

[pause]

The answer is A.

Now we are ready to start.

After you have listened once, replay each recording.

[pause]

One: What interest rate did the man's investment receive this year?

[pause]

Man: I'd like some advice about my investment in Lawsons. I was hoping for five per cent but it didn't even repeat last year's four point five per cent.
Woman: Well, four per cent's not all that bad the way things are at the moment. A lot of companies are giving far less.

[pause]

Two: Which aspect of company policy are staff unhappy about?

[pause]

Woman: Staff are very unhappy about our changes in policy on this.
Man: Well, things aren't all bad. They've just had a pay rise.
Woman: But they always saw staff development as essential for their jobs, especially those who're applying for higher positions in the company.
Man: We're starting various courses as soon as the budget allows. Don't they know that?

[pause]

Three: How does the man feel about moving offices?

[pause]

Man: We're relocating during the week starting July the twelfth.
Woman: That's going to be a bit tight, isn't it, Paul?
Man: We'll all just have to make sure we've got a good plan and inform everyone well in advance.
Woman: That's easier said than done.
Man: It'll be fine – don't worry.

[pause]

Four: Which graph shows profits at AJB?

[pause]

Man: The profits for AJB look rather disappointing, don't they?
Woman: You're right. The problems really started when Baileys opened up in the UK earlier this year. What do you think will happen next year?
Man: Well, the forecast was good until these figures were announced. But predictions are much less positive now.

[pause]

Five: What percentage of the woman's MBA fees will the company pay?

[pause]

Woman: I'd like to know about the company's educational awards for MBA courses. I have heard you usually pay fifty per cent.
Man: That is for staff with over five years' service. Staff who have been with us for two to five years, as in your case, get thirty-five per cent, while those with less than two years' service get twenty-five per cent.
Woman: I see. Thank you.

[pause]

Six: Where is the GNZ Communications stand?

[pause]

Woman: I wonder if you could help me. I'm looking for the GNZ Communications stand. Is it on this floor?
Man: Yes. Go left here, past the Homes Two Thousand and Twenty exhibition. Turn right after the café, walk straight ahead and you'll see GNZ on your left, opposite Smart Systems – near the lifts.
Woman: Thank you.

[pause]

Seven: What time does the man expect to arrive at the meeting?

[pause]

Man: Hello Liz. It's Mark. I'm still at the airport. The plane's delayed. I was supposed to be at the meeting at twelve thirty but I'm probably not going to make it until thirteen thirty. We are not scheduled to take off for another hour yet, so won't land till eleven forty-five at the earliest.
Woman: Don't worry. I'll send your apologies.

[pause]

Eight: Which chart shows the company's current income by country?

Key

[pause]

Man: The sales figures look very good.
Woman: Yes, Germany has done very well again with sales up to eleven million pounds. But the overall increase was largely due to excellent sales in Italy and Greece. We'd forecast eleven million for Italy but, in fact, they overtook Germany, almost reaching thirteen million, while Greek sales were up by over three million to eight million.
Man: That's interesting.

[pause]

That is the end of Part One.

[pause]

Part Two. Questions 9 to 15.

Look at the notes below.

Some information is missing.

You will hear a man giving some information about a conference.

For each question 9–15, fill in the missing information in the numbered space using a word, numbers or letters.

After you have listened once, replay the recording.

You have ten seconds to read through the notes.

[pause]

Now listen, and fill in the missing information.

Woman: SmartTarget Marketing Division. Sarah Marks speaking.
Man: Hello, my name's Tim Adams. I'm calling to let you know about this year's GlobalNet Conference next month from the twenty-fifth to the twenty-seventh of November.
Woman: Oh yes. It was at the University Conference Centre last year, wasn't it?
Man: That's right. This year it's on at the International Conference Centre. It's much bigger this year, you see.
Woman: Will there be more seminars, then?
Man: More of everything. Five hundred and thirty-five exhibitors and over one hundred and fifty free seminars. We have some really exciting guest speakers this time.
Woman: Oh yes. Such as?
Man: Well, Mike Daughton, Director of InfoSoft UK, will give the opening presentation.
Woman: Mike Dalton?
Man: No, Daughton, D-A-U-G-H-T-O-N.
Woman: Oh, of course. That should be interesting. What time are the seminars on?
Man: The conference centre is open from nine thirty to six thirty and the seminars run from ten thirty to five thirty. All the seminars are listed in the programme.
Woman: And how much are the tickets?
Man: If you book now it'll be three hundred and twenty-five pounds. Otherwise, it'll be one hundred and twenty-five pounds per day on the door.
Woman: How can I register?
Man: You can either register online or call the booking office on 0-1-double-4-3-double-7.
Woman: Great. Thanks for your call.

[pause]

Now listen to the recording again.

[pause]

That is the end of Part Two. You now have ten seconds to check your answers.

[pause]

Part Three. Questions 16 to 22.

Look at the notes about the career of Steven Jackson.

Some information is missing.

You will hear part of a presentation given by Steven Jackson at an interview.

For each question 16–22, fill in the missing information in the numbered space using one or two words.

After you have listened once, replay the recording.

You have ten seconds to read through the notes.

[pause]

Now listen, and fill in the missing information.

[pause]

Man: I have always enjoyed working in marketing and research, and I think I have gained a very good knowledge of the skills necessary to do a job effectively. At the moment, I'm working as a Research Manager. Energy and ideas are very important, and in my present employment I've shown that I have these qualities. The company deals in the production of building equipment and I've been with them for five years now. I'm sure you have heard of my present company, Standard Construction. My position involves finding out about the latest scientific developments. I have a good academic background in this field and graduated in Chemistry from London University fourteen years ago.

One thing I particularly enjoy about my present job is travelling, mainly in Europe and the United States. I meet representatives of other companies and discuss new ideas for the use of new materials in construction. It's very important to know what is happening in other countries like Germany and France.

Before this, I was Marketing Assistant for a Spanish plastics company for four years. My knowledge of different languages and cultures has been a great advantage, and I plan to learn German as well. At the moment, I regularly do business in French and Spanish, and travel widely in Europe including frequent visits to Sweden and Holland, where my business is all done in English.

I plan to leave my present job before the end of the year. There are several projects I have to finish in October and November. If I were offered a post here I would be available to begin in December.

I want to work for a company that has ambitions to be a world leader in its field, which is why I'm applying for this position.

[pause]

Now listen to the recording again.

[pause]

That is the end of Part Three. You now have twenty seconds to check your answers.

[pause]

Part Four. Questions 23 to 30.

You will hear a discussion between James, the General Manager, and Sarah, the Office Manager, of a company.

For each question 23–30, mark one letter (A, B or C) for the correct answer.

After you have listened once, replay the recording.

You have forty-five seconds to read through the questions.

[pause]

Now listen, and mark A, B or C.

Man: Come in, Sarah.
Woman: Thanks.
Man: Right. We need to discuss some of the issues raised at the last meeting with your department.
Woman: Yes, there were a lot of questions about computer systems and flexible working hours.
Man: We'll talk about computer systems in a minute, but I think we can leave flexible working hours for the time being. What I'm really very concerned about at the moment, though, is how some staff are working. I'm not at all happy with how long it's taking for some reports on visits to come in. Peter Jones, for instance, hasn't produced a single report on time. The last, on his visit to Berlin was two weeks late. It's not as though they're long reports – they should only take a short time to write.
Woman: I'll certainly warn Peter about getting reports in more quickly but it really comes down to a question of staff training. I think we need to do some workshops on time management.
Man: I agree, but getting consultants in to do the training costs money. It'd be cheaper to use one of our own staff. Have we got anyone who could do it?
Woman: Laura Williams has some management training experience.
Man: She's away on a team building course at the moment, though, isn't she?
Woman: Only 'till next week. I'll speak to her when she gets back. I'm sure she'll be interested.
Man: Now, I'd like to move on to computer systems. As you know, we're going to upgrade our software. The plan was to install it in January but that's proved difficult so it's going in during February because we certainly want it to be ready and running for March.
Woman: Good. I'm worried about the computer skills of some of the staff, though. A few could do with some extra training.
Man: I'm sure you're right. Could we organise that on the premises, do you think?
Woman: Possibly, but it'd be expensive. I know the business college in Park Street has a really good computer section. I've compared their prices with those of the computer training centre at Blackstone and the college prices are far more reasonable.
Man: Let's go for that, then. Will you see to it?
Woman: Certainly. Now, I think this would be a good time to make some office changes before the new software comes in. The Accounts team need a bigger office. At the moment, we've only got five people using the Marketing office on the second floor, so Accounts could take over that office if we moved Marketing to the first floor.
Man: And Human Resources up to the third floor? Yes, that sounds a good idea.
Woman: Great. It'll mean moving a lot of equipment. Accounts keep complaining about

Key

some of their equipment. It'd be nice if we could replace it.
Man: We certainly can't replace all of it. What's causing most problems?
Woman: Well, we've had to call technical support in at least once every week for the past two months to deal with the fax machine. The printers were causing trouble but they're working well enough now and everyone complains that the photocopier is slow but it's alright, really.
Man: Right, I'll see what we can do. Now, I have to go in a minute. What do we need to discuss when we meet next week?
Woman: There's the Health and Safety report.
Man: Oh, John Wilkins has already done that.
Woman: Good. What about the programme for the French clients? They're coming at the beginning of next month.
Man: Time is getting short. We'd better deal with that.
Woman: And then what about getting a new PA to replace Louise?
Man: Oh, we can leave that, I think. She isn't going till the end of April now.
Woman: That's good. I thought she was leaving sooner.

[pause]

Now listen to the recording again.

[pause]

That is the end of Part Four. You now have ten minutes to transfer your answers to your Answer Sheet.

[pause]

Note: Teacher, stop the recording here and time ten minutes. Remind students when there is **one** minute remaining

That is the end of the test.

Test 3   Reading

Part 1

1 A   2 A   3 C   4 C   5 A

Part 2

6 G   7 E   8 F   9 D   10 H

Part 3

11 F   12 C   13 D   14 H   15 A

Part 4

16 B   17 C   18 A   19 A   20 C
21 B   22 A

Part 5

23 B   24 C   25 C   26 A   27 A
28 B

Part 6

29 B   30 C   31 A   32 C   33 C
34 A   35 C   36 B   37 A   38 C
39 B   40 B

Part 7

41 EDINBURGH
42 3/THREE
43 (MS, ETC.) GILLIAN ROLLAND
44 (A) SCREEN
45 (£)400/FOUR HUNDRED (POUNDS)

Test 3   Writing

Part 1

Sample A

> I write you because I will attend in a seminar next week. I think it's interesting because it refers to our actually job.
>
> I suggest that you could be interested and we could travelling together. I wait your answer.
>
> Best regards
>
> Chris

Band 3
As the purpose of the seminar is not stated, the first content point has not been addressed. However, the other points are clear and the language is appropriate to the task, and it is written in an appropriate register.

Sample B

> There will be a seminar about new recruitment ways. I think you could be interested in attending it as you've just got this position as Human Resources consultant. Would you like to travel with me?
>
> Please answer me ASAP

Band 5
All the content points are clearly covered and there is evidence of a good range of language, with minimal errors. Overall, the effect on the reader is very positive.

Part 2
Sample C

> Dear Mr Davis,
>
> Thank you for your fax. I'm very pleased to stay in your hotel. The service in your hotel is very good. But the business facilites, in the hotel are : less professional than others; : And some equipment is in shortage. But I think it still as room for improvements.
>
> This time I am going to stay in Great Hotel in the city centre due to the venue of the conference is in downtown. And I will accept the company car you offered. I am looking forward to see you.
>
> Yours faithfully,
>
> Weija Chang

Band 2
From the candidate's answer, it is clear that s/he did not fully understand the task, so despite reasonable language control and a range of appropriate expressions and suitable register, the reader would be confused as to the purpose of the fax. Consequently, a higher mark could not be awarded.

Sample D

> Dear Mr Davis
>
> Im reference to your fax, the Sation Hotel is not bad, but the Palace Hotel is better. The problem of the Station Hotel is that the conference room is too small and there aren't enough suports to do a presentation. Also the staff is rude.
>
> The Palace Hotel is more for business people and they have a great conferance room.
>
> It would be fantastic if a company car can pick up me at the airport on the 28th August. At the time I'll arrive it's difficult to find taxis.
>
> Thank you very much
>
> Yours Sincerelly
>
> BH

Band 5
All the content points are clearly covered, and effective use is made of a good range of grammar and vocabulary. There are a number of minor errors, but these do not impede the communication of the message.

Test 3   Listening

Part 1
1 B   2 B   3 A   4 A   5 C   6 A
7 C   8 B

Part 2
9 SHAPPEN
10 28(TH) (OF) JUNE
11 5450
12 RACHEL
13 FTZ079
14 (£)17,250
15 163B

Part 3
16 FINANCE COMPANY/FINANCIAL COMPANY
17 (OF) RETAIL (CHAIN)
18 (IN) GERMANY
19 (GRADUATE) TRAINING
20 (HIS) (MY) ASSISTANT
21 FURNITURE (RANGE)
22 POWERHOUSE (GROUP)/POWER(-)HOUSE (GROUP)

Part 4
23 A   24 C   25 B   26 B   27 C
28 A   29 C   30 A

Tapescript

Listening Test 3

This is the Business English Certificate Preliminary 3, Listening Test 3.

Part One. Questions 1 to 8.

For questions 1–8, you will hear eight short recordings. For each question, mark one letter (A, B or C) for the correct answer.

Here is an example: Who is Emily going to write to?

[pause]

Key

Man: Emily, that supplier we use has become very unreliable, and we've decided to look for another one.
Woman: Seems a good idea.
Man: We don't need to inform our clients, but could you send a note round to all our departments when we've decided who to replace the supplier with?
Woman: Yes, of course.

[pause]

The answer is A.

Now we are ready to start.

After you have listened once, replay each recording.

[pause]

One: What does George think about the new company magazine?

[pause]

Woman: What do you think about the new company magazine, George?
Man: It looks very professional, but I think they could have done it more cheaply.
Woman: But don't you think people will find it useful?
Man: Well, they might find it interesting but that's not the same thing, is it?

[pause]

Two: In which product range are sales growing most quickly?

[pause]

Man: The sales figures for this year are excellent, aren't they?
Woman: Yes. All the new lines are performing very well indeed.
Man: I didn't think things like video recorders would sell so well.
Woman: No, but in fact sales of home entertainment products are rising the fastest.
Man: Faster than kitchen goods?
Woman: Faster than everything, even stationery.

[pause]

Three: Which set of information is unavailable?

[pause]

Woman: Have you finished getting the information about best performance yet? I'd like to use it at tomorrow's meeting if possible.

Man: Nearly. The data on individual sales personnel isn't all in yet.
Woman: What about product categories? That's more important.
Man: No problem with that, or with the highest performing stores. I've put the figures on your desk.
Woman: Thanks.

[pause]

Four: Where is the Human Resources department?

[pause]

Man: Excuse me, is Human Resources on this floor?
Woman: No, you're on the wrong floor – it's on the next one up. You can take the lift or use the stairs at the end of the corridor. It's just past the Marketing offices, which are on the left when you come out of the lift.

[pause]

Five: Which hotel are they going to book for Mr Sands?

[pause]

Woman: Which hotel shall we book Mr Sands into?
Man: Well, the Westgate's close to us but it doesn't offer value for money compared to the Laurel or the Crown.
Woman: But the Laurel's farther away from the office than the Crown. And we stopped using the Crown because there were too many problems.
Man: OK. Since it's a short visit, let's choose the nearest one.

[pause]

Six: Why is the man phoning?

[pause]

Woman: Good morning, Swiftcom.
Man: Hello, this is Martin Smithers. I'm ringing about an appointment with Peter Field.
Woman: Oh yes, Peter's sorry he couldn't make a definite arrangement yesterday. He had to check his diary about the fourth.
Man: Is it OK?
Woman: Well, that or the ninth.
Man: The fourth suits me better.
Woman: Fine, I'll tell him.

[pause]

Seven: How much does the man earn in total at the moment?

[pause]

Woman: You obviously want to know about the salary we'd pay. You'd earn forty thousand pounds a year. How does that compare with your present salary?
Man: Well, with commission I make forty-six thousand pounds but the basic salary is thirty-five thousand pounds.
Woman: I see. Well, if you decide to take the post we can review your salary after a six-month trial period.

[pause]

Eight: Which graph shows the company's future sales targets?

[pause]

Woman: So, what are your targets for the next three years?
Man: Well, we think the huge investment in the advertising campaign this autumn will take sales to one point five million dollars in Year One – in other words, next year. That level should then hold steady, with a slight drop predicted in Year Three.

[pause]

That is the end of Part One.

[pause]

Part Two. Questions 9 to 15.

Look at the form below.

Some information is missing.

You will hear a man phoning the Human Resources department of the company where he works.

For each question 9–15, fill in the missing information in the numbered space using a word, numbers or letters.

After you have listened once, replay the recording.

You have ten seconds to read through the notes.

[pause]

Now listen, and fill in the missing information.

[pause]

Woman: Human Resources.
Man: Hello, Neil Andrews here. I understand you've managed to recruit a new assistant for my office?
Woman: Oh yes, Neil – would you like to take down the details?

Man: Please. Can I have her surname?
Woman: Well, it's Shappen, S-H-A-double-P-E-N, and it's Ms.
Man: That's an unusual name. OK. Now, can she begin on the fourth of July, as I requested?
Woman: Ah, good news there. We've actually been able to bring that forward to the twenty-eighth of this month.
Man: June? Oh, that's great. We're so busy, it'll make a real difference.
Woman: I've got everything set up for her.
Man: A phone line?
Woman: Yes, and she'll be on extension five-four-five-o. We've used all the five-four-fours.
Man: Oh right. And what about email?
Woman: Easy. Her address'll be Rachel – that's R-A-C-H-E-L . . .
Man: . . . and then at horsham-dot-com.
Woman: Yeah, as normal. We haven't got any other Rachels. And then there's her password . . .
Man: Oh, for the network?
Woman: Uh-huh, it's F-T-Z-O-seven-nine.
Man: Oh, mine's just numbers.
Woman: We've got a new system now.
Man: I see. And her pay?
Woman: Yes, she'll be on grade C, to begin with, that's seventeen to nineteen and a half thousand – she'll be getting seventeen thousand, two hundred and fifty.
Man: Fine. Well, I'd like to send her a letter to welcome her.
Woman: Good idea. She lives at a hundred and sixty-three-B, West Street. That's in Kenford.
Man: OK, thanks a lot.
Woman: No problem.

[pause]

Now listen to the recording again.

[pause]

That is the end of Part Two. You now have ten seconds to check your answers.

[pause]

Part Three. Questions 16 to 22.

Look at the notes about a designer.

Some information is missing.

You will hear part of a speech by a designer who is accepting an award.

For each question 16–22, fill in the missing information in the numbered space using one or two words.

Key

After you have listened once, replay the recording.

You have ten seconds to read through the notes.

[pause]

Now listen, and fill in the missing information.

[pause]

Man: Ladies and gentlemen. I'm delighted to receive this award from the UK design industry and am grateful to everyone involved.

My career has come a long way since I started my first job as a junior employee in a finance company. I worked in that field for fifteen years, changing companies several times. However, in nineteen eighty-nine a recruitment consultancy contacted me with an invitation to join a retail chain . . . as a senior manager, and I accepted.

It was the right choice – within two years I'd moved into fashion design. My early creations were mostly unsuccessful and when the company attended the London Design Exhibition, none of my work was included. However, the following year my designs were shown at another trade fair in Germany; they received a lot of attention and sales increased. There were many opportunities open to me, especially in the US, so I decided to set up my own business.

I always try to have original ideas, to be ahead of the field. Last year, of course, I received the Conrad Prize for the graduate training scheme we introduced, but until this award I had never previously won anything for my fashion designs.

I'd like to thank someone who's been very important to me since I started the company . . . that's my assistant, who plays a part not just in the design department, but also in planning, marketing and recruitment.

I certainly hope this award will help us to grow. We're planning expansion into areas other than clothing design, including textiles and kitchen equipment. We've also just started working on a contract we have with a Swedish manufacturer for a new furniture range, and we've recently acquired a partner company – our Eye for Design name won't change – but we're working closely with the Powerhouse Group on a range of lighting equipment, something which hopefully will bring us . . .

[pause]

Now listen to the recording again.

[pause]

That is the end of Part Three. You now have twenty seconds to check your answers.

[pause]

Part Four. Questions 23 to 30.

You will hear Janet Willis, a management consultant, advising David Smith, a managing director, about using a marketing services agency.

For each question 23–30, mark one letter (A, B or C) for the correct answer.

After you have listened once, replay the recording.

You have forty-five seconds to read through the questions.

[pause]

Now listen, and mark A, B or C.

Woman: In our last meeting, David, we talked about the need for bringing in agency staff to take over the marketing strategy.

Man: Yes. I've talked it over with my senior management team. It's not something we'd considered before and we're not sure this is the right moment for a commitment like that.

Woman: I would say this is the perfect moment. The business is doing really well and you are ahead of the competition but this means there are new challenges ahead. Your managers are already so busy due to the recent expansion that I think your day-to-day business could suffer if you don't get outside help.

Man: I see. How would an agency be able to help us develop our business?

Woman: Well, when I discussed with the marketing team their plans for a new marketing strategy, I felt their ideas lacked imagination and creativity. I'm not sure that they have the resources or the experience to take the business forward. And besides, I don't think recruiting new people to the team is the answer at this stage as this would be expensive and time-consuming. Consultants, though, are experts at providing solutions quickly, which is what you need most of all.

Man: And what type of agency do you have in mind for this?

Woman: You can go for the safe option and choose a well-known agency such as Walker Taylor, but they would be very expensive. An agency like Duffy and Partners on the other hand is smaller but has the relevant experience and employs some of the best consultants.

Man: I have heard that Red Ribbon is very good.

Woman: That's true, but they're not really specialists in your field.

Man: Anyway, before we decide which agency to use, we need to decide what we'd want them to do.

Woman: There are two ways to use an agency: to do a specific job, like an audit or product launch, or to involve them in the long-term development of your business, which is what I would do in your situation.
Man: It sounds like an expensive long-term commitment to me.
Woman: It needn't be. There are ways to limit the costs. Before you draw up the contract you must decide what your aims are and only agree to pay according to how well the agency achieves these aims. Most agencies will agree to terms like this these days.
Man: I like the sound of that. I'd feel I was really getting value for money.
Woman: Remember though, David, it's up to you as well to make it work. Successful relationships depend on sharing information about the business freely and being totally open with the agency. Then let them get on with their job without trying to take control and don't waste time on unnecessary meetings.
Man: Mm.
Woman: Things can go wrong, of course, even when your whole team's involved in the process. Agencies frequently complain that a key reason for failure is that middle managers are sometimes too afraid to say yes to new ideas because saying no is less risky.
Man: I can see that. So, you're saying that we have to be good clients if we want to achieve good results?
Woman: Exactly. In my experience, great clients get great agencies. They understand that, if the business is successful, then the agency is successful.
Man: Well. It's something I need to think about. I agree we should certainly meet some of these agencies and see what they have to offer. But I know the marketing team won't like it.

[pause]

Now listen to the recording again.

[pause]

That is the end of Part Four. You now have ten minutes to transfer your answers to your Answer Sheet.

[pause]

Note: Teacher, stop the recording here and time ten minutes. Remind students when there is **one** minute remaining.

That is the end of the test.

Test 4 Reading

Part 1
1 C   2 A   3 B   4 C   5 B

Part 2
6 D   7 E   8 G   9 B   10 A

Part 3
11 G   12 F   13 H   14 C   15 E

Part 4
16 A   17 B   18 C   19 B   20 B
21 A   22 C

Part 5
23 C   24 C   25 B   26 A   27 C
28 A

Part 6
29 B   30 C   31 C   32 A   33 B
34 A   35 C   36 C   37 A   38 B
39 B   40 A

Part 7
41 (MR) JIM MOORE
42 COLSTON NEWLAND
43 PERFECT PRESENTATIONS
44 (FAST-TRACK [OPTION]) HALF (A) DAY/ 1/2 (A) DAY
45 (A) BANK TRANSFER

Test 4 Writing

Part 1

Sample A

> Dear Bob
>
> I work in the headquarter and have some problems to start the consolidation program. I have got the following error message "There is not enough space".
>
> Could you please check that for me?
>
> Thanks
>
> Claudia

Key

Band 4
All the content points have been achieved in this response, but the request does not communicate sufficient urgency for this to gain the top band.

Sample B

> Hello Bob
>
> In the Quality dept. where I work, we have a problem with our computers. From Monday we have not been able to log on the MRB program.
>
> Can you please come and repear this as soon as possible.
>
> Regards

Band 5
This is a very good attempt at the task set, achieving all content points. No effort is required by the reader.

Part 2
Sample C

> Re: 50th Anniversary Celebration
>
> Dear Mrs Johannson
>
> We will invite you to our birthday event. Our company is 50 years old! The event take place on Saturday the 19 December 2004. We have quote a lot of attractions. For example it come a star as a guest speaker but we do not say who it is. You can happend to a lot other attractions, Do you come to the event and let you surprise. We have two overtime accommodation. The hotel "Florida" or the "Stella" hotel.
>
> If you have any questions, please do not hesitate to contact me.
>
> Yours sincerely
>
> Ingrid Keller
>
> International sales department

Band 2
This is an inadequate attempt at the task. Although the first and last sentences are clear and well written, the numerous impeding errors in the rest of this response would confuse the reader.

Sample D

> Dear Mrs Johannson
>
> I am happy to tell you, that we do for our 50th anniversary celebration an event and that we include you to come to it.
>
> This event would be on the 20th November in our company.
>
> On the event we will presentate you our new ideas for a faster and better working your orders. Another point on the agenda is, that you can tell us, what you dislike on our work.
>
> Please let me know, if you want to come untill the 10th November.
>
> Your sincerely
>
> Jarek Kretowicz

Band 3
This is a reasonable achievement of the task set. The fourth content point relating to overnight accommodation is missing, and there are a number of errors, but overall this response displays adequate range of structure and vocabulary.

Test 4   Listening

Part 1

1 A   2 B   3 B   4 C   5 B   6 C
7 B   8 C

Part 2

9 34
10 BARRINGTON
11 RAINAWAY
12 170
13 11
14 15
15 472993

Part 3

16 COMPUTER GAMES/PRODUCTS
17 (AN) ENGINEERING (COURSE)
18 SALES MANAGER
19 CUSTOMER SERVICE(S)
20 CAREER
21 EXECUTIVE DIRECTOR
22 (TV) ADVERTISING/
   ADVERTISEMENT(S)/ADVERTS/ADS

Part 4

23 A	24 C	25 B	26 A
27 B	28 B	29 B	30 C

Tapescript   Starts at track 38 – 49
Listening Test 4

This is the Business English Certificate Preliminary 3, Listening Test 4.

Part One. Questions 1 to 8.

For questions 1–8, you will hear eight short recordings. For each question, mark one letter (A, B or C) for the correct answer.

Here is an example: Who is Emily going to write to?

[pause]

Man: Emily, that supplier we use has become very unreliable, and we've decided to look for another one.
Woman: Seems a good idea.
Man: We don't need to inform our clients, but could you send a note round to all our departments when we've decided who to replace the supplier with?
Woman: Yes, of course.

[pause]

The answer is A.

Now we are ready to start.

After you have listened once, replay each recording.

[pause]

One: When will the meeting take place? 39

[pause]

Man: I'm afraid we have to change the date of the next marketing meeting. Unfortunately, the US manager can't make June the fifteenth now.
Woman: So when are you suggesting?
Man: Well, could you do either June the twelfth or the twenty-third instead?
Woman: I suppose so, though neither is terribly convenient.
Man: Let's go with the earlier date then – don't want to leave it too long.

[pause]

Two: Which part of the woman's computer is causing a problem? 40

[pause]

Woman: Hi, it's Jane. I'm having a bit of trouble with my computer again.
Man: Right. Is it the same problem?
Woman: No, the screen's fine now, but nothing happens when I press the keys on my keyboard.
Man: What about the mouse?
Woman: It reacts OK to the mouse.
Man: Fine, I'll come and have a look.

[pause]

Three: Which chart shows last year's sales figures?

[pause]

Woman: The first quarter was disappointing, but thanks to an excellent advertising campaign, sales recovered in the second quarter and reached over seventy million by the end of the year. The drop in the third quarter was due to seasonal factors.

[pause]

Four: What is the lowest price the man can buy the machine for?

[pause]

Woman: ... and this machine is fifteen thousand dollars.
Man: What does that include?
Woman: Free servicing for a year. Free training. Plus you can exchange it for a newer model after two years, for just ten thousand dollars.
Man: Would you give us a discount?
Woman: I could say fourteen five hundred.
Man: I was hoping to pay less. Thirteen thousand?
Woman: Sorry. That's our best price.

[pause]

Five: What will help the company to increase production?

[pause]

Man: I expect you're all celebrating, aren't you? I hear you've had a huge new order?
Woman: Well, yes ... but resources are a problem. We've got to increase production, and staff are already doing overtime. So, we're cutting down on the packaging to push things through faster.
Man: Couldn't you take on temporary staff?
Woman: We considered that, but decided against it in the end.

[pause]

Key

Six: Which chart shows the company's spending on training last year?

[pause]

Woman: Looking at the three main areas of spending, we can see that language training, normally our biggest expense, was overtaken last year by IT and pushed into third place by Health and Safety, which now has greater importance.

[pause]

Seven: Where should staff leave office cars?

[pause]

Woman: Do you know about the new arrangements for office cars?
Man: I always park them on the road outside.
Woman: Well, now we have to leave them on-site behind the building.
Man: What about the keys? I left them in the car last time I parked on the premises.
Woman: The gates are locked at night, but it's probably safer to leave them in the box outside Reception.

[pause]

Eight: Who does the man think will get the job?

[pause]

Woman: . . . three people have applied for the new post, Rachel, Anna and Laura.
Man: Anna's only been here a year . . . I'm sure Laura will get it . . . she's been here five years. She's also well liked . . .
Woman: Mm . . . Rachel is too, but she's fairly new, as well . . .
Man: True. Perhaps she and Anna will be promoted when they have more experience . . .

[pause]

That is the end of Part One.

[pause]

Part Two. Questions 9 to 15.

Look at the notes below.

Some information is missing.

You will hear Ann Simpson of Blackwell Sports talking to a journalist.

For each question 9–15, fill in the missing information in the numbered space using a word, numbers or letters.

After you have listened once, replay the recording.

You have ten seconds to read through the notes.

[pause]

Now listen, and fill in the missing information.

[pause]

Woman: Publicity . . . Ann Simpson.
Man: It's Jonathon Timms from *Business News*. I'm calling to get some information for my article on major sport companies . . .
Woman: Ah yes. How can I help?
Man: Well, facts and figures really. Blackwell have had a great year, haven't they?
Woman: Yes, our turnover is up to one hundred and forty-six million pounds, that's a thirty-four million pound increase.
Man: Is that due to the merger I've read about?
Woman: That's right. We now own Barrington Outdoor Equipment . . .
Man: That's spelt . . . ?
Woman: B-A-double-R-I-N-G-T-O-N.
Man: Thanks. It's been a good year for camping equipment, then?
Woman: Yes. Our new tent, the Rainaway, has sold well.
Man: Sorry . . . ?
Woman: Rainaway. That's R-A-I-N-A-W-A-Y.
Man: Oh, I see . . . thanks. Is it sold in all your stores in the UK?
Woman: Yes. It is now. To begin with, it was only available in our ten London stores but now it's sold in our hundred and seventy outlets throughout Britain.
Man: How many of those opened this year?
Woman: Well, we opened twelve between the first of March and the thirtieth of September, and there'll be another eleven opening in the New Year.
Man: Your original market was women's sports clothing. How are sales there?
Woman: Excellent – they represent forty-five per cent of our clothing sales – that's up from thirty per cent eighteen months ago . . . a fifteen per cent rise.
Man: Great. I think I have everything I need now . . .
Woman: Good, but if you need to contact me again, my mobile number is O-seven-seven-nine-O-four-seven-two-double-nine-two, no sorry, that last number's three.
Man: Many thanks.
Woman: You're welcome.

[pause]

Now listen to the recording again.

[pause]

That is the end of Part Two. You now have ten seconds to check your answers.

[pause]

Part Three. Questions 16 to 22.

Look at the notes about an American businessman called Matthew Webb, who is working in the UK for a company called Electra.

Some information is missing.

You will hear part of a presentation describing his working life.

For each question 16–22, fill in the missing information in the numbered space using one or two words.

After you have listened once, replay the recording.

You have ten seconds to read through the notes.

[pause]

Now listen, and fill in the missing information.

[pause]

Man: I discovered at an early age that I only did well at something if I enjoyed doing it. I didn't like maths at school so I never got good results, but sport was different. So, now I work for Electra, a company selling computer games, I understand very well that the most important thing for our sales is that our customers are happy using our products!

My first job after leaving school was in a bike shop. Then, I decided to go to college to study engineering, but I soon gave that up because I couldn't get enthusiastic about it. After that, I got a job working as a rep for a frozen food company, which was much better than studying. Our main customers were a convenience store chain called Star Stores, and the people there seemed to like the way I worked, as later they offered me the job of sales manager. I really enjoyed my time there and I managed to increase market share considerably by improving customer service. I stayed with them for ten years before moving to join Electra.

Although at first I earned less money, I knew in the long term the move to Electra was important for my career development. I started working with the staff, showing them how to deal with the customers – a happy customer always returns to the store! That's how I was promoted to the job of training organiser for the USA, working with the new staff. Now I'm here in the UK, I am an Executive Director.

Although we haven't introduced any new products yet, our sales figures have improved due to increased TV advertising. We're opening six new stores next year and although I'm busy, I enjoy feeling I'm part of the company's success story.

[pause]

Now listen to the recording again.

[pause]

That is the end of Part Three. You now have twenty seconds to check your answers.

[pause]

Part Four. Questions 23 to 30.

You will hear a radio interview with Beth Hatfield, the Director of Jumpstart, a recruitment agency.

For each question 23–30, mark one letter (A, B or C) for the correct answer.

After you have listened once, replay the recording.

You have forty-five seconds to read through the questions.

[pause]

Now listen, and mark A, B or C.

Man: Welcome to *Business Start-ups*. Our guest today is Beth Hatfield. Beth started her own recruitment agency for temporary marketing staff when she lost her own job some years ago. Thank you for coming, Beth.
Woman: Thank you, John. Nice to be here.
Man: A lot of people think it's the end of the world when they lose their job. Tell us what happened in your case . . .
Woman: Well, I was working for Fast Forward, a marketing services agency. It seemed very successful – you know, with a very impressive client list . . . but I had heard there were cash flow problems. There was some talk of a possible takeover to save the company, but this all came to nothing. Without any notice, we were all suddenly made redundant.
Man: And how did you react?
Woman: Well, I didn't think that there'd be any difficulty for me, or for the friends I'd worked with at the agency, in finding new jobs. My main

139

Key

concern was actually for one of the company's main clients, Dryden Limited.
Man: The agricultural machinery company?
Woman: Yes, that's right. I was running their big sales campaign for Eastern Europe, and the promotion still had another six months to run. Now they'd be left without an agency, I felt very bad about that.
Man: And it was because of this that you started up your own business?
Woman: Yes. I talked to them and offered to run the account from home. I already had a small PC and a fax machine and plenty of room to work in, but nothing suitable for running such a large campaign.
Man: And did they invite you to work at their offices?
Woman: I really wanted to work from home, so they gave me an up-to-date computer and a photocopier. And that was the beginning of Jumpstart, my own agency. I soon had too much to do so I took on an assistant. She's still with me.
Man: What happened next?
Woman: A friend of mine, Thomas Beck, gave me some really useful advice. He's a successful investment manager – I've known him for years.
Man: What did he suggest?
Woman: Well, I had a lot of plans for Jumpstart, offering a whole range of marketing services. Thomas liked my ideas, but he thought I should focus on just one area.
Man: And did you take his advice?
Woman: Yes, I decided to make Jumpstart a marketing recruitment agency, because I knew the business and had good contacts.
Man: Was it easy getting started? How did you raise the money?
Woman: Well, I'd learnt an important lesson from my time at Fast Forward. They'd had to stop trading because of large bank loans. I didn't want to make the same mistake with Jumpstart. I thought I might have to sell my house, but, fortunately, somebody I'd worked with at Fast Forward was very interested in coming in with me as a partner and also had money to invest.
Man: So how did Jumpstart find enough recruits to get started?

Woman: We planned to advertise in local newspapers because it was so cheap, but then decided that it wouldn't reach the right people, so we placed ads in several specialist marketing magazines. Expensive, but very effective – lots of enquiries. Nowadays we advertise mainly on the internet, but not then, of course.
Man: And what do you look for in a recruit? What is essential?
Woman: Well, even though the work is temporary, I've always felt that it's very important to provide quality staff. Because of this, I don't think it really matters if the recruit has a degree in marketing, for example, but I always insist on them having experience in the field. Location is never a problem though – I recruit staff for companies all over the country.
Man: You make it sound easy. Weren't there any problems?
Woman: It wasn't difficult getting good recruits, though it took up a lot of time. What wasn't easy at first was selling the idea of temporary marketing staff to possible clients. The real challenge however, was negotiating rates that companies would see as value for money. They were quite used to going to an agency for temporary secretaries but not for other types of staff.
Man: Well, your efforts really worked. Now, tell us, what plans . . .

[pause]

Now listen to the recording again.

[pause]

That is the end of Part Four. You now have ten minutes to transfer your answers to your Answer Sheet.

[pause]

Note: Teacher, stop the recording here and time ten minutes. Remind students when there is **one** minute remaining.

That is the end of the test.

INTERLOCUTOR FRAMES

To facilitate practice for the Speaking test, the scripts that the interlocutor follows for Parts 2 and 3 appear below. They should be used in conjunction with Tests 1–4 Speaking tasks. These tasks are contained in booklets in the real Speaking test.

Interlocutor frames are not included for Part 1, in which the interlocutor asks the candidates questions directly rather than asking them to perform tasks.

Part 2: Mini presentations for two candidates (about five minutes)

Interlocutor:
- Now, in this part of the test I'm going to give each of you a choice of two different topics. I'd like you to choose one topic and give a short presentation on it for about a minute. You will have a minute to prepare this and you can make notes if you wish.
- All right? Here are your topics. Please don't write anything in the booklet.

[Interlocutor hands each candidate a booklet and a pencil and paper for notes.]

Interlocutor:
- Now *B*, which topic have you chosen, A or B?
- Would you like to show *A* your task and tell us what you think is important when *[interlocutor states candidate's chosen topic]*?

[Candidate B speaks for one minute.]

Interlocutor:
- Thank you. Now, *A*, which do you think is most important, *[interlocutor reads out bullet points]*?
- Thank you. Now *A*, which topic have you chosen, A or B?
- Would you like to show *B* your task and tell us what you think is important when *[interlocutor states candidate's chosen topic]*?

[Candidate A speaks for one minute.]

Interlocutor:
- Thank you. Now *B*, which do you think is most important, *[interlocutor reads out bullet points]*?
- Thank you.
- Can I have the booklets, please?

Part 3: Collaborative task and discussion (about five minutes)

Interlocutor:
- Now, in this part of the test you are going to talk about something together.
- I'm going to describe a situation.

Example: The manufacturing company you work for wants to improve contacts with a local business college. Talk together for about two minutes about some of the ways the company could help the college and decide which two are best.

- Here are some ideas to help you.

[Interlocutor places the booklet in front of the candidates so that they can both see it.]

- I'll describe the situation again.

Example: The manufacturing company you work for wants to improve contacts with a local business college. Talk together for about two minutes about some of the ways the company could help the college and decide which two are best.

Now talk together. Please speak so that we can hear you.

[Candidates have about two minutes to complete the task.]

- Can I have the booklet, please?

[Interlocutor selects one or more of the following questions as appropriate.]

Example:
- Can you think of any other things a company could do to help a local college? (Why?)
- How important do you think practical experience is for business students? (Why?/Why not?)
- What do you think are the advantages to a college of having contacts with local businesses? (Why?/Why not?)
- Do you think there are advantages to a company in having contacts with a local college? (Why?/Why not?)
- Do you think the skills people learn in one company are always useful in another company? (Why?/Why not?)

Thank you. That is the end of the test.

Sample Answer Sheet: Reading

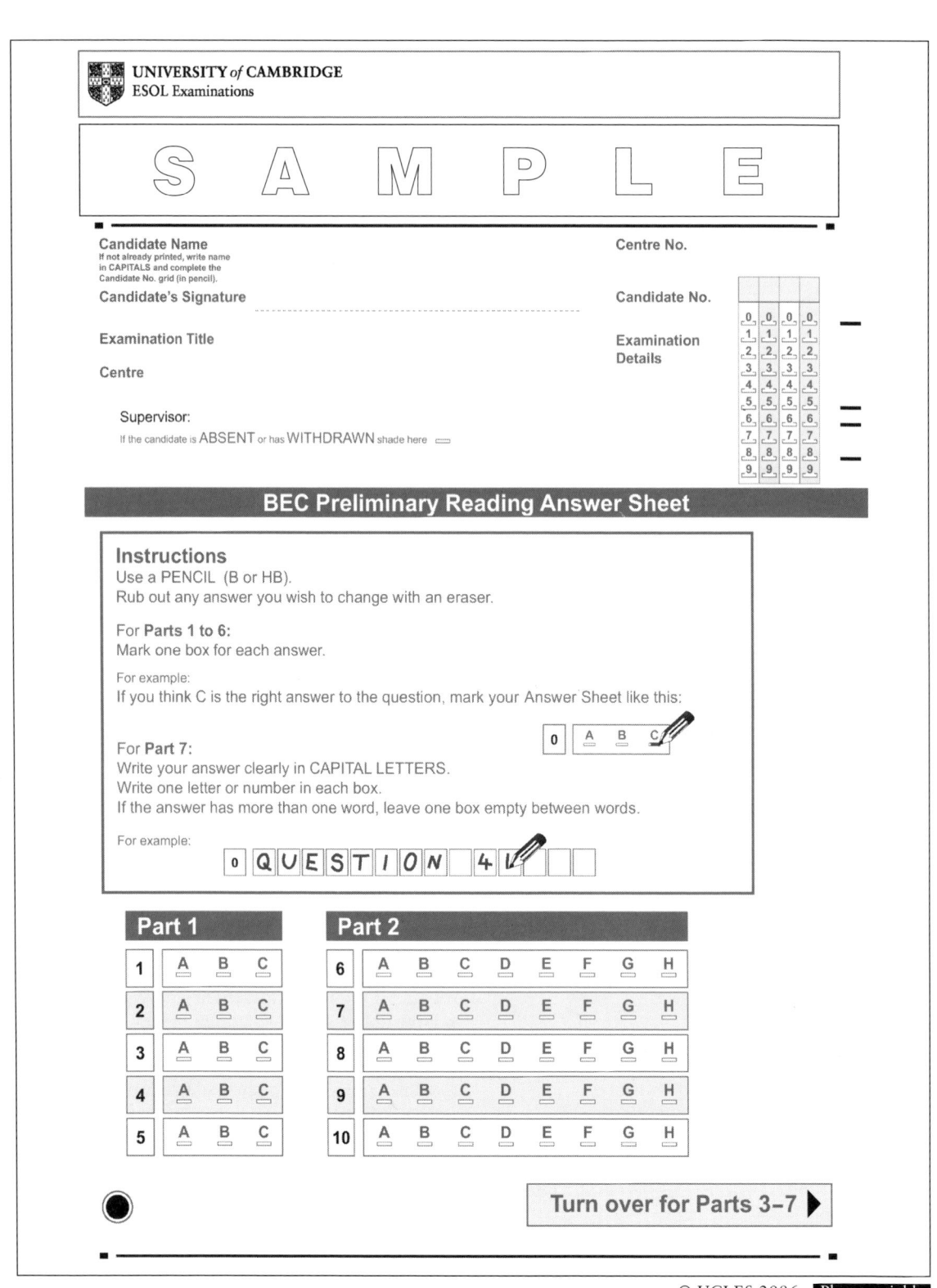

UNIVERSITY of CAMBRIDGE
ESOL Examinations

SAMPLE

Candidate Name
If not already printed, write name in CAPITALS and complete the Candidate No. grid (in pencil).

Candidate's Signature ....

Examination Title

Centre

Supervisor:
If the candidate is ABSENT or has WITHDRAWN shade here

Centre No.

Candidate No.

Examination Details

BEC Preliminary Reading Answer Sheet

Instructions
Use a PENCIL (B or HB).
Rub out any answer you wish to change with an eraser.

For **Parts 1 to 6:**
Mark one box for each answer.

For example:
If you think C is the right answer to the question, mark your Answer Sheet like this:

`0  A  B  C`

For **Part 7:**
Write your answer clearly in CAPITAL LETTERS.
Write one letter or number in each box.
If the answer has more than one word, leave one box empty between words.

For example:

`0  Q U E S T I O N   4`

Part 1

1	A B C
2	A B C
3	A B C
4	A B C
5	A B C

Part 2

6	A B C D E F G H
7	A B C D E F G H
8	A B C D E F G H
9	A B C D E F G H
10	A B C D E F G H

Turn over for Parts 3–7 ▶

© UCLES 2006   Photocopiable

142

Sample Answer Sheet: Reading

Part 3

11	A	B	C	D	E	F	G	H
12	A	B	C	D	E	F	G	H
13	A	B	C	D	E	F	G	H
14	A	B	C	D	E	F	G	H
15	A	B	C	D	E	F	G	H

Part 4

16	A	B	C
17	A	B	C
18	A	B	C
19	A	B	C
20	A	B	C
21	A	B	C
22	A	B	C

Part 5

23	A	B	C
24	A	B	C
25	A	B	C
26	A	B	C
27	A	B	C
28	A	B	C

Part 6

29	A	B	C		33	A	B	C		37	A	B	C
30	A	B	C		34	A	B	C		38	A	B	C
31	A	B	C		35	A	B	C		39	A	B	C
32	A	B	C		36	A	B	C		40	A	B	C

Part 7

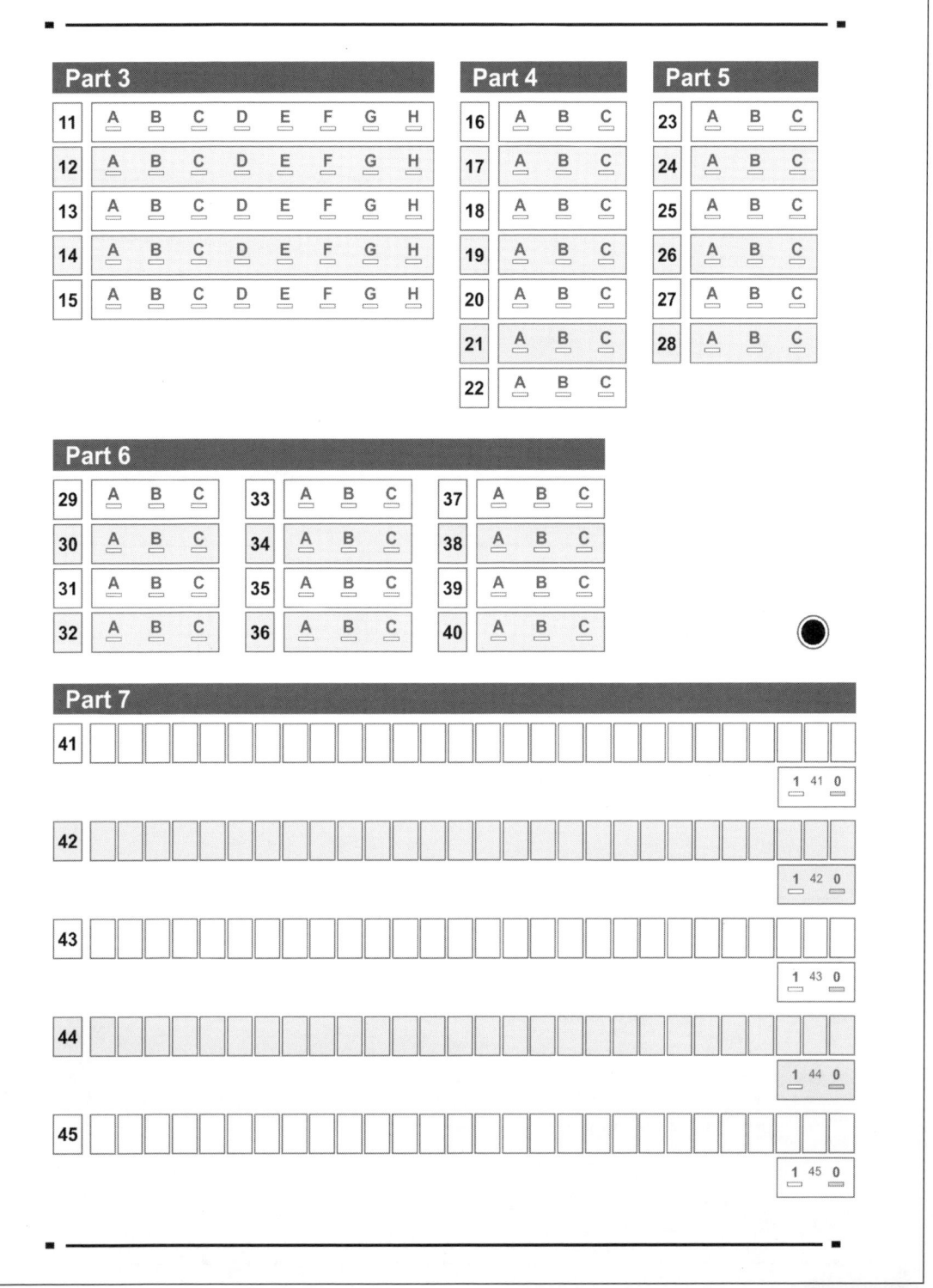

41	
42	
43	
44	
45	

© UCLES 2006 Photocopiable

Sample Answer Sheet: Writing

UNIVERSITY of CAMBRIDGE
ESOL Examinations

SAMPLE

Candidate Name
If not already printed, write name in CAPITALS and complete the Candidate No. grid (in pencil).

Candidate's Signature

Examination Title

Centre

Supervisor:
If the candidate is ABSENT or has WITHDRAWN shade here

Centre No.

Candidate No.

Examination Details

BEC Preliminary Writing Answer Sheet

Part 1: Write your answer in the box below.

Write your answer to Part 2 on the other side of this sheet ▶

This section for use by Examiner only

Part 1   0   1   2   3   4   5

© UCLES 2006   Photocopiable

Sample Answer Sheet: Writing

Part 2: Write your answer in the box below.

This section for use by Examiner only											
Part 2	0	1.1	1.2	2.1	2.2	3.1	3.2	4.1	4.2	5.1	5.2

Examiner Number

0 1 2 3 4 5 6 7 8 9
0 1 2 3 4 5 6 7 8 9
0 1 2 3 4 5 6 7 8 9
0 1 2 3 4 5 6 7 8 9

Examiner's Signature

© UCLES 2006 Photocopiable

Sample Answer Sheet: Listening

BEC Preliminary Listening Answer Sheet

Instructions
Use a PENCIL (B or HB).
Rub out any answer you wish to change with an eraser.

For **Parts 1 and 4**:
Mark one box for each answer.
For example:
If you think C is the right answer to the question, mark your Answer Sheet like this:

For **Parts 2 and 3**:
Write your answer clearly in CAPITAL LETTERS. Write one letter in each box.
If the answer has more than one word, leave one box empty between words.
For example:

`0 | Y | O | U | R |   | A | N | S | W | E | R |   |`

Part 1

1. A B C
2. A B C
3. A B C
4. A B C
5. A B C
6. A B C
7. A B C
8. A B C

Part 2

9.
10.
11.
12.
13.
14.
15.

Turn over for Parts 3 and 4 ▶

© UCLES 2006 Photocopiable

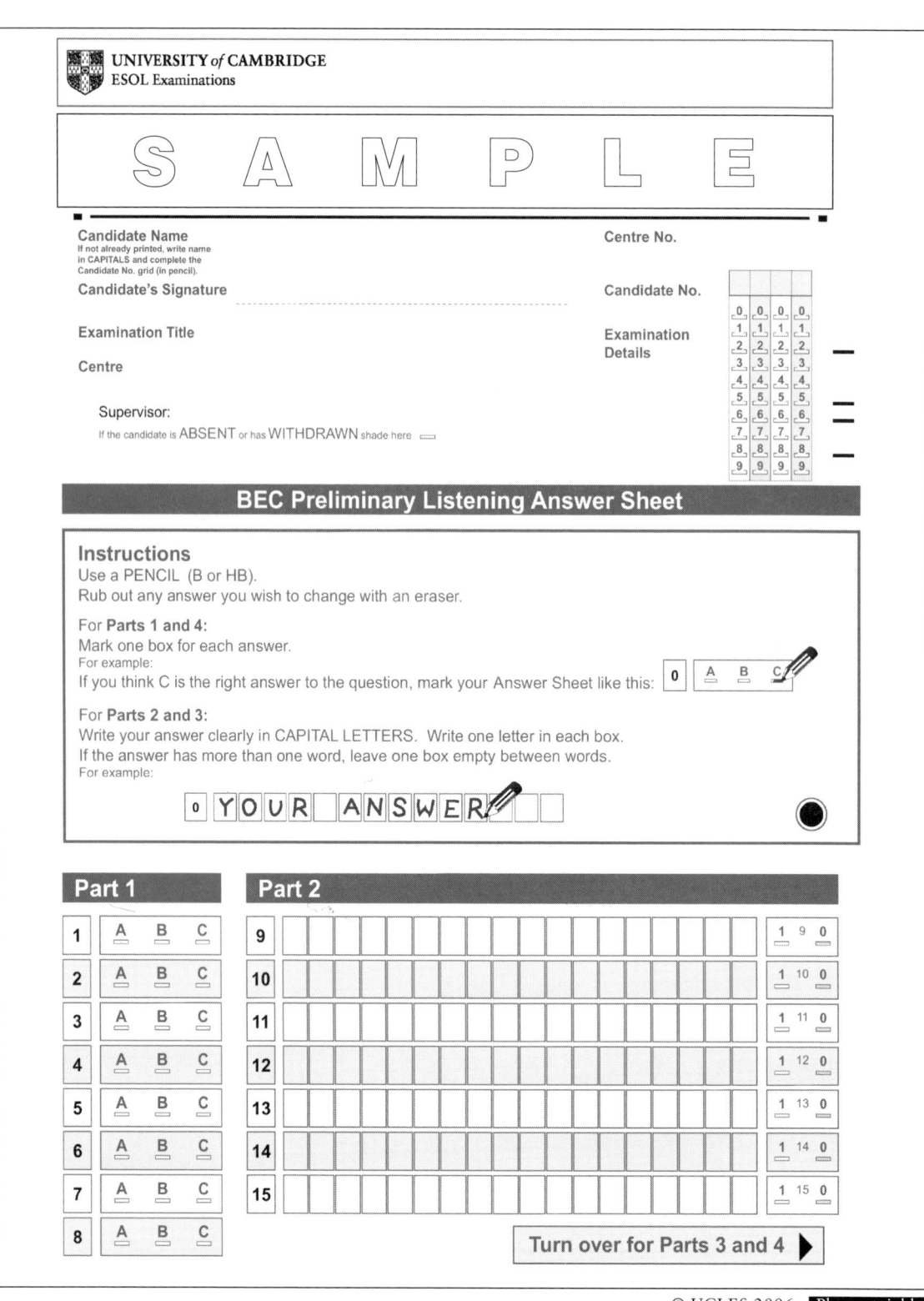

Sample Answer Sheet: Listening

Part 3

16.
17.
18.
19.
20.
21.
22.

Part 4

23. A B C
24. A B C
25. A B C
26. A B C
27. A B C
28. A B C
29. A B C
30. A B C